RED ARMY WEAPONS OF THE SECOND WORLD WAR

RED ARMY WEAPONS OF THE SECOND WORLD WAR

MICHAEL GREEN

Pen & Sword
MILITARY

First published in Great Britain in 2022 by
PEN & SWORD MILITARY
an imprint of Pen & Sword Books Ltd
Yorkshire – Philadelphia

ISBN 978-1-39909-538-9

Typeset by Concept, Huddersfield, West Yorkshire, HD4 5JL.
Printed and bound in England by CPI Group (UK) Ltd, Croydon CR0 4YY.

Pen & Sword Books Ltd incorporates the imprints of Aviation, Atlas, Family History, Fiction, Maritime, Military, Discovery, Politics, History, Archaeology, Select, Wharncliffe Local History, Wharncliffe True Crime, Military Classics, Wharncliffe Transport, Leo Cooper, The Praetorian Press, Remember When, White Owl, Seaforth Publishing and Frontline Books.

For a complete list of Pen & Sword titles please contact
PEN & SWORD BOOKS LTD
47 Church Street, Barnsley, South Yorkshire, S70 2AS, England
E-mail: enquiries@pen-and-sword.co.uk
Website: www.pen-and-sword.co.uk
or
PEN & SWORD BOOKS
1950 Lawrence Rd, Havertown, PA 19083, USA
E-mail: uspen-and-sword@casematepublishers.com
Website: www.penandswordbooks.com

Contents

Dedication

The author would like to dedicate this work to fellow author Ian V. Hogg (1926–2002), who served for twenty-seven years in the British Army and eventually retired as a Master Gunner at the Royal Military College of Science. His numerous books, dating back to the 1960s, inspired an early interest in military weaponry by this author and his subsequent career as a military history and military technology writer.

Foreword

During the First World War in an oft-told story, Russian infantrymen were on the line when an aeroplane flew overhead. They quickly fired upon the plane, shooting it down. There was no way it could be a Russian plane because the Russians were not smart enough to build something so complicated.

With the above story as a tongue-in-cheek backdrop, *Red Army Weapons of the Second World War* is a marvellous read and probably Mike Green's most difficult work to date. For well over the twenty years that I have known and read Green's work, his books have usually focused on one area such as tanks, artillery, submarines or weapons in a specific war. In *Red Army Weapons of the Second World War*, however, the author tackles not just light, medium and heavy tanks but adds infantry weapons, artillery, mechanization and Lend-Lease equipment in what is his finest and most comprehensive work on an army and its equipment, and the problems faced with production and its use. Throughout this very important work, the reader should ask themselves if the Red Army was learning lessons or simply repeating mistakes.

The Red Army and its drive to mechanization and modernization was a trial filled with starts and stops, political interference, production problems, doctrinal and organizational issues and an almost continuous state of war – internal and external. At the centre of the drive to modernization was a conflict within the army over operations, doctrine, tactics and the use of tanks in a war of the future, the role of artillery and infantry in relation to tanks, and the role of tanks as infantry support weapons or independent forces or a part of the artillery.

Red Army Weapons of the Second World War begins with the first tanks acquired by the Red Army – those captured from the 'White' forces during their civil war, mostly First World War-era British tanks – and ends with the employment of the T-34/85 during the Second World War. During this time period, the Soviet Union underwent fundamental changes throughout all strata of the country. This would affect the Red Army, and production facilities were also not immune.

To say that this is a good book is an understatement. The author once again shines as he deftly weaves a narrative through the political, military and industrial land mines through the use of military reports, papers and articles. This book is a masterpiece and fills an important place in our historiography of the weapons of war. A commander once asked a historian 'What do we have left to learn about WWII?' The historian responded with 'a lot'.

Randy R. Talbot, Command Historian (Retired)
US Army Tank-automotive and Armaments Command (TACOM)

Acknowledgements

As with all published works, authors depend on many friends for assistance in reviewing their material. These include Peter Shyvers, Alex Zaretser, Oleg Sapunkov and Michael Panchyshyn. A particular word of thanks also goes to Sherman tank researcher/historian Joe DeMarco for his assistance. A great many of the photographs come from the Dreamstime stock photo agency with a smaller number from PICRYL, which labels itself as 'The World's Largest Public Domain Site'. Several friends also contributed photographs and are credited in the captions.

Note to the Reader

Due to the book's size and format, this work is only a very broad overview of the subject. Some of the more obscure weapons do not appear due to reasons of space. Weights appear in American short tons.

Chapter One

Infantry Weapons

The Red Army, officially known as the Workers' and Peasants' Red Army (in the Russian language abbreviated to RKKA), entered into the Second World War (1 September 1939 to 2 September 1945 and known to Russians as 'The Great Patriotic War') with a wide range of infantry weapons.

Revolver

The oldest infantry weapon employed by the Red Army in the Second World War was the seven-round Nagant M1895 revolver. It fired a 7.62×38mmR round. The suffix letter 'R' signifies that the cartridge cases were rimmed, meaning that the rim of a cartridge is larger in diameter than the base of the cartridge case. This revolver came in two versions: a single- and a double-action model. Production of the single-action model continued until 1918 and the double-action model lasted in production until 1942. The revolver first saw combat with the Russian Army during the Russo-Japanese War (8 February 1904 to 5 September 1905).

The effectiveness of pistols is summed up by weapons expert Ian V. Hogg in his book *The Encyclopedia of Infantry Weapons of World War Two*: 'A British general once said that he had seen thirty men wounded by pistol fire during the course of World War Two, of which twenty-nine were his own troops who had inadvertently shot themselves while cleaning or otherwise mishandling their pistols.'

Automatic Pistol

The Red Army's replacement for the Nagant M1895 revolver appeared as an eight-round semi-automatic pistol commonly referred to as the Tokarev. It began showing up in Red Army service in the early 1930s. In contrast to the revolver, the semi-automatic pistol fired a 7.62×25mm rimless round. A significant advantage with rimless ammunition is that the cartridge cases slide more easily across one another when feeding into the weapon from a magazine.

The initial version of the Tokarev automatic pistol bore the designation TT-30, with an improved model labelled the TT-33. Sources cite that between 1931 and 1945 more than a million were produced by Soviet industry. From a book titled *Allied Infantry Weapons of World War 2* is the following extract on the TT-33:

> The 7.62mm TT-33 was based on the well-tried Colt-Browning designs with some variations all its own such as the hammer mechanism. Once in production, it became apparent that the design still had some faults ... The main faults of the T-33 were a tendency for the eight-round box magazine to fall out of the butt unexpectedly and a short service life before the mainspring

fractured. These problems had been eliminated by 1941. Thereafter the TT-33 proved to be a reliable and sturdy weapon.

Bolt-Action Rifles

Before and during the Second World War, the Red Army's standard rifle was the bolt-action Mosin-Nagant M1891/30. As of 1924, the Red Army began referring to the weapon as the Mosin after the weapon's main designer Sergei Mosin, an officer in the Imperial Russian Army.

The prefix number '1891' in the rifle's designation refers to the original design date of the gun in question. The suffix number '30' represents the year (1930) in which the modified and improved version of the rifle entered into production. The 9lb M1891/30 rifle had a five-round magazine and a length of 48.5in.

The M1891/30 rifle fired the powerful 7.62 × 54mmR cartridge. The suffix size measurement describes the length of the cartridge case. Due to its length, it proved a clumsy weapon to use in close-quarter fighting. An unwieldy 17in-long spike bayonet compounded its clumsiness. Adding to the rifle's shortcomings were a poorly-designed bolt-action and safety mechanism.

Nevertheless, the M1891/30 rifle had its fans. In the book *Panzer Killers: Anti-Tank Warfare on the Eastern Front*, a Red Army soldier stated: 'If it comes to the weapon I liked, then, of course, it would be our Mosin 1890/30 rifle. It was utterly reliable. You could drag it through sand, clean it, and keep firing. Its bullet keeps its stopping power out to 5 kilometres [about 3 miles].'

The 1891/30 rifle's simplicity allowed Soviet factories to build 13 million examples. However, despite the numbers manufactured, there were never as many as the Red Army needed.

Sniper Mosin-Nagant

By the early 1930s, the Red Army began fielding a sniper version of the M1891/30 rifle fitted with optical scopes copied from German designs. In this new configuration it had a specially-made bolt handle bent down to accommodate the optical scopes. Assembly of the sniper rifle began in 1937.

In the book titled *The Mosin-Nagant Rifle* is the following description of the roles of Red Army snipers:

> First, the sniper was to undertake counter-sniping work to destroy any assets that could disrupt the advance of their own troops. Second, the sniper was to destroy the enemy command structure by killing commanders at all levels. Third, the sniper was to destroy enemy soldiers conducting fire, such as artillery forward observers.

In a translated article by Sergey Kiyatkin that appeared in a Russian magazine on Red Army sniper rifles is the following passage on the ammunition they employed:

> During World War II, Soviet snipers used the following ammunition: 7.62mm rifle cartridges with light, heavy, armour-piercing (B-30), armour-

piercing incendiary (B-32), sighting and incendiary (PZ) and tracer (T-46) bullets. Cartridges with light and heavy bullets, as a rule, were used for firing at enemy manpower … Cartridges with an incendiary bullet were used to set fire to objects that interfere with observation and shelling of sheltering snipers, as well as wood-and-earth firing points of the enemy; cartridges with a tracer bullet – for target designation (and only in the offensive).

Grenade-Launcher

In the late 1920s, the Red Army fielded the Dyakonov grenade-launcher for the M1891/30 rifle. It could fire a fragmentation grenade, a coloured signal grenade and a flare grenade. Unfortunately, the grenade-launcher proved to be unreliable and ineffective in combat, subsequently disappearing from service between 1941 and 1942.

The same grenade-launcher was reissued late-war with the advent of a shaped charge (hollow charge) anti-tank grenade. However, due to its lack of lethality, it was unpopular with Red Army infantrymen. They preferred much more effective captured German hand-held anti-tank weapons such as the *Panzerschreck* or *Panzerfaust*.

A Training Problem

Despite its straightforward design, riflemen issued with the Model 1891/30 rifle needed a training period to make effective use of it. Because the German Army invasion of the Soviet Union beginning on 22 June 1941 resulted in the loss of so many Red Army infantry divisions – 100 out of 178 – the Red Army infantrymen mustered in the months after the invasion often went into combat with little or no training on rifles and, in some cases, without a gun.

In his book *My Just War: The Memoir of a Jewish Red Army Soldier in World War Two*, Gabriel Temkin recalls being sent into battle for the first time without a weapon and never having been trained to use a rifle:

> The *politruk* [political officer] was right. There were plenty of rifles, ammunition and hand grenades left by the dead and wounded in the field and trenches, and I was soon to 'learn on the job' how to use them. I had not seen yet the first sunrise on the bridgehead when, before daybreak, and with no support from our artillery behind the river, our company was rushed into an attack on enemy positions. We were led by a junior lieutenant … We were supposed to engage in a hand-to-hand fight and, as soon as we passed the barbed wire, everybody on our side began shooting wildly. I did likewise, not aiming at anybody or anything in particular because visibility was poor, and even if it were excellent, I would not have performed any better as I never practised shooting from a real rifle to a target. Be that as it may, the Germans were not caught by surprise. Their heavy machine guns began to crackle and mowed down our soldiers.

A More Practical Mosin-Nagant Rifle

The Red Army recognized by the late 1930s that the existing 48.6in M1891/30 rifle was too long to be practical for infantry support troops such as machine-gunners or mortarmen. Therefore a shorter 40in version of the rifle designated the M38 Carbine (which lacked a bayonet) went into production.

The popularity of the M38 Carbine led to its occasional employment by riflemen in place of the rifle. Eventually, a carbine version of the M91/30 appeared equipped with a folding spike bayonet. It became the M44 Carbine and found its way to some Red Army infantrymen in place of their M1891/30 rifles.

Semi-Automatic Rifles

The first semi-automatic (self-loading rifle) in Red Army service was the Fedorov Avtomat. It had a twenty-five-round curved box magazine and fired a rimless Japanese-made 6.5 × 50mm round. Designed before the First World War for the Russian Imperial Army, only 100 examples saw service in the conflict.

Fedorov Avtomat production began for the Red Army in 1924, but ended in October the following year as the Red Army decided to forgo weapons using foreign ammunition. Approximately 3,200 examples of the weapon came off the factory floor before going into storage. The First Soviet-Finnish conflict (30 November 1939 to 13 March 1940), known as the 'Winter War', resulted in the reissue of the Fedorov Avtomat to the Red Army.

Next-Generation Semi-Automatic Rifles

In 1936, after the Fedorov Avtomat, the Red Army took into service the semi-automatic Simonov AVS-36 rifle. It came with a fifteen-round box magazine and fired the 7.62 × 54mmR cartridge. However, an overly complex design led to the Red Army pulling the weapon from service in 1940 with about 65,000 built.

The replacement for the 7.62mm AVS-36 was the Tokarev SVT-38. The first examples appeared in Red Army service in 1939. Large-scale production began the following year. It came with a ten-round box magazine and fired the same 7.62 × 54mmR round as the AVS-36.

The shortcomings of the SVT-38 appear in a book titled *Allied Infantry Weapons of WW2*: 'it was prone to an alarming number of breakdowns caused by the inevitable knocks of service life, extreme cold and the ingress of dirt.'

Keep Trying

The Red Army soon ordered a simplified, supposedly more reliable version of the SVT-38 with the provision for a bayonet, and assigned it the designation SVT-40. The weapon had a length of 49.6in. In the May 1946 issue of the American military publication *Intelligence Bulletin* is the following passage on the weapon:

> The Russian Tokarev Semi-Automatic Rifle, M1940, is a 7.62 millimeter (cal. .30) gas-operated, air-cooled, magazine-fed shoulder weapon ... Workmanship in the rifle is good, but it lacks the ruggedness that is evident in US

design [M1 Garand]. This is primarily due to the Soviet attempt to make a rifle of light weight. In order to eliminate extra weight, the barrel and receiver are manufactured from very thin stock. The receiver walls are very easily bent, putting the weapon out of action … Fifty rounds fired in continuous bursts will generally ruin the rifle. The stock, too, has been made of light woods and is kept dry rather than oiled. All this has resulted in a rifle of lightweight – only 8.6 pounds with an empty magazine.

The Red Army eventually decided that the SVT-40 was unreliable, too costly and time-consuming to build in large numbers. Thus production came to an end in 1942 after about a million examples came out of the factories.

In addition to the standard SVT-40, the Red Army had industry come up with a sniper model. Testing of the weapon showed that it was unsuitable for the role due to round dispersion problems caused by design flaws with the rifle and scope mount. Solving the weapon's problems would have required significant rifle and scope mount changes, so the Red Army cut their losses and cancelled further development.

Automatic Rifle

A fully-automatic version of the SVT-40, designated the AVT-40, saw limited production starting in the summer of 1942. However, firing high-power 7.62×54mmR rounds from the AVT-40 in full auto led to problems with controllability. The recoil-generated stress also proved more than the weapon could handle. This issue and others led to the gun's cancellation by the Red Army within a year.

On the Tank Archives blog hosted by Peter Samsonov is the following translated passage on the conclusions from a wartime Red Army report on the AVT-40:

1. Due to the decreased combat usefulness, conversion of a semi-automatic rifle to a fully automatic one is not rational.
2. In order to reach required density of fire with a high probability of hitting the target, it is better to use submachine guns, which have the advantages of simpler production, higher reliability, compactness, high magazine capacity, larger stocks of ammunition, etc.

Submachine Guns

The first service iteration of a submachine gun (SMG) for the Red Army was the selective-fire Degtyaryov PPD 34 that entered service in 1935. The PPD-34 was copied from the design of a post-First World War German SMG.

The PPD-34 fired the same rimless 7.62×25mm pistol ammunition used in the TT-30 and TT-33 automatic pistols. An advantage for the Red Army was that pistol ammunition was cheaper to make than rifle rounds as it used fewer strategic resources.

Only 4,000 examples of the PPD-34 were built due to the Red Army's senior leadership not seeing a requirement for SMGs. In a short-sighted move, they had all their PPD-34s placed into storage in 1939. However, the Finnish Army's successful use of submachine guns in the Winter War led to the reissue of the PPD-34 in 1940.

In its original configuration, the PPD-34 came with a curved twenty-five-round box magazine. An improved version labelled the PPD-34/38 featured a Soviet industry-designed drum magazine holding seventy-three rounds. The Red Army was impressed by the seventy-one-round drum magazine of the Finnish Army KP/-31 Suomi submachine gun, so they had it copied by Soviet industry for the PPD-34/38.

Simplified Submachine Guns

The Red Army demanded a more cost-effective and simpler to build SMG and pushed Soviet industry to come up with a redesigned and improved selective-fire model of the PPD-34/38, referred to as the PPD-40. As with the previous submachine guns, they were made of good-quality steel.

Approximately 90,000 examples of the roughly 8lb PPD-40 came off the assembly lines between 1940 and 1941, with the Finnish-inspired drum magazine bringing the weapon's weight up to about 12lb.

The Red Army eventually concluded that the PPD-40 remained too complicated and hence too costly to build in the immense numbers it needed. Therefore a redesigned and simplified version took its place on the factory floor and received the designation PPSh-41. Sources cite a figure of 5 million examples of the weapon built during the war. Some late-production PPSh-41s were capable of only fully-automatic fire.

The selective-fire PPSh-41 retained the seventy-one-round drum magazine of its predecessors and had a rate of fire ranging between 600 and 900 rounds per minute. In comparison, the German Army MP-40 had a rate of fire between 500 and 550 rounds per minute and the American M1A1 Thompson between 600 and 700 rounds per minute. The PPD-40 was about 31in long, with the PPSh-41 33.2in in length.

In the 31 December 1942 American military publication titled *Tactical and Technical Trends* is a passage on the PPSh-41: 'According to a Russian instructional poster, best results are obtained with this weapon as follows: single shot, up to about 300 yards; short bursts, about 200 yards; long bursts, about 100 yards.'

For the Red Army, the widespread use of the PPSh-41 solved a critical problem. As a point-and-shoot weapon, it required little training for the individual Red Army soldier to become proficient in its use, while mastering a rifle required a certain degree of training and time which proved difficult for the Red Army to provide.

In *Russian Combat Methods in World War Two* written by German officers postwar is the following passage: 'The best weapon of the Russian infantryman was the machine pistol [submachine gun]. It was easily handled, equal to Russian winter conditions, and one which the Germans also regarded highly. This weapon was slung around the neck and carried in front on the chest, ready for immediate action.'

Some 34 per cent of the 23 million rifles and SMGs built by Soviet industry during the war years were SMGs. In contrast, of the approximate 12 million rifles and SMGs constructed by German industry, only 11 per cent were the latter, although Second World War movies and television series often portray almost every other German soldier having a submachine gun.

Magazine Problems

Despite the PPSh-41's overall reliability, replacement drum magazines proved problematic for Red Army soldiers due to poor quality control at the factories. The result was mismatched tolerances between magazine wells and drum magazines, forcing the typical Red Army infantryman to experiment with different drum magazines until he could find those that fit his particular weapon.

While the drum magazine of the PPSh-41 provided a great deal of firepower for individual Red Army soldiers, its reloading process proved difficult and time-consuming. The drum magazine also showed itself to be easily damaged in the field. Another problem was that Soviet industry could never build enough of them as quickly as needed due to their complexity.

As a replacement for the sometimes troublesome seventy-one-round drum magazine of the PPSh-41, a thirty-five-round box magazine appeared in 1942. Early-production examples of the box magazine proved too fragile, and in November 1943 a stouter, more durable version entered production. Unfortunately, the problem of mismatched tolerances between magazine wells and the box magazines also led to issues for Red Army soldiers trying to find examples that fit the gun with which they were issued.

Another issue with the new box magazine for the PPSh-41 was that the weapon's high fire rate emptied the box magazine very quickly if not monitored by the user. Despite the box magazine's introduction, the heavy and bulky drum magazines remained in use until the end of the Second World War and beyond.

An Even Simpler Submachine Gun

The Red Army identified a requirement in 1942 for a new, more compact, lightweight and even simpler and more cost-effective SMG than the PPSh-41. The answer was the roughly 7lb PPS-42 approved for production in July 1942, with manufacture beginning in September 1942 and about 47,000 coming out of the factories. The weapon was basically made of stamped heavy-gauge metal parts that even less well-equipped factories could manufacture.

The PPS-42 was chambered to fire the 7.62×25mm round and capable of automatic fire only, unlike the previous SMGs that could fire single shots if required. The rate of fire of the PPS-42 was limited to between 400 and 500 rounds per minute to improve controllability. It fired from a very reliable thirty-five-round box magazine that tended to fit the magazine wells of the PPS-42.

To reduce the weapon's 35in length, it had a simple folding metal stock that brought its length down to 25in.

An improved version of the PPS-42 appeared in 1943 as the PPS-43, with around 2 million examples coming out of the factory doors by 1946. However, despite the advantages offered by the PPS-42/43 over the PPSh-41, so many Soviet factories were already committed to building the PPSh-41 that the PPS-42/43 remained only a supplement to the PPSh-41 and never became its replacement.

In the US Army translation of the Red Army's official manual on the PPS-43 submachine gun is the following extract on the weapon's merits by the Soviet designer of the AK-47:

> It can be said in all seriousness that A.I. Sudayev's submachine gun, created and issued to the Red Army beginning in 1942, was the best submachine gun of the World War II period. Not one foreign design could be compared with its simplicity of construction, reliability, durability in function and ease of use. Airborne troops, tankers, scouts, partisans and ski troops loved the Sudayev weapon for its high tactical, technical and combat qualities, combined with its small dimensions and weight.

Light Machine Gun

The Red Army's infantry squad-level machine gun was the DP-28, serviced by a two-man crew. The air-cooled weapon entered service with the Red Army in 1928 and fired the 7.62×54mmR round from a forty-seven-round horizontal pan magazine. That specific design feature earned it the nickname of 'the Record Player' from Red Army personnel.

With only six moving parts, the DP-28 machine gun proved highly reliable in most regards. It weighed about 20lb and had a rate of fire between 500 and 600 rounds per minute. The weapon had a removable barrel, but it was not considered a quick-change barrel as the second man in the team did not carry a spare barrel. Rather, the barrel was removable so it could be cleaned.

Early-War Red Army Squad Organization

In the book titled *Barbarossa: German Infantryman vs Soviet Rifleman* by David Campbell, he breaks down the arrangement of a Red Army infantry squad in 1941:

> By 1941, the basic infantry unit was an 11-man squad containing a squad leader, a two-man LMG [light machine gun] team, two submachine-gunners and six riflemen. The squad leader, LMG assistant and the riflemen were each armed with the M1890/30 Mosin-Nagant rifle, or – supplies permitting – the SVT-40 semi-automatic rifle; the LMG gunner carried a DP-28 light machine gun and the submachine-gunners carried PPD-38/40s.

The design drawbacks of the DP-28 included the horizontal pan magazine's fragile construction and a mainspring that could fail during prolonged firing due to heat build-up.

A later model of the DP-28 designated the DPM, with the suffix letter 'M' standing for modification, corrected some of the original version's design issues but retained the horizontal pan magazine.

Due to wartime shortages of the infantry squad model of the DP-28 and DPM, a modified version of the DT tank version of the weapon found its way into infantry use. Infantrymen appreciated the DT's thicker barrel which allowed more prolonged firing, as well as its larger sixty-round horizontal pan magazine.

Medium Machine Guns

The oldest machine gun in service with the Red Army during the Second World War was the water-cooled Maxim Model 1910/30. It used the 7.62×54mmR round that fed into the weapon with a cloth belt, thereby avoiding the problem of rim lock which occurs when the rim of one cartridge locks together with another, thereby jamming a weapon's feed mechanism.

With a rate of fire of between 520 and 580 rounds per minute, the rugged firing mechanism of the Maxim Model 1910/30 made it highly reliable throughout its service career with the Red Army. It initially saw combat with the Red Army in its original configuration during the First Russo-Finnish War.

Due to its roughly 50lb weight and size, the Maxim Model 1910/30 rode on a small two-wheeled metal carriage typically fitted with a thin armoured shield. The carriage weighed about 100lb and served as the weapon's firing platform. In the book titled *Infantry Weapons* by author John Weeks appears the following extract:

> These small wheeled carriages are fine so long as one is traveling along hard roads or tracks, but come to mud or ditches or sand, and the gun crew then had to carry the gun and carriage. Even the Russian peasant must have found the 152lbs a tall order to hump about.

The Intended Replacement

Despite its yeoman service with the Red Army during the Second World War, the Maxim Model 1910/30 was obsolete. The original replacement, the air-cooled Degtyaryov M1939 'DS', fired the same 7.6×54mmR round. However, it had a couple of serious design problems that included out-of-battery detonations and the round extraction process. These issues led the Red Army to discontinue production of the weapon shortly after the German invasion with around 10,000 examples constructed.

The follow-on to the M1939 DS was the air-cooled Goryunov SG-43. Like its predecessors, the belt-fed SG-43 fired the 7.62×54mmR round and fell within a medium machine-gun classification. It had a rate of fire of between 500 and 700 rounds per minute.

The SG-43 had a reliable and straightforward design. It moved around the battlefield with the aid of a small two-wheeled metal carriage with an armoured shield. The SG-43 on its two-wheeled carriage came in at around 90lb. Unfortunately Soviet industry could not build enough of the new medium guns (74,000) to replace all the Maxim Model 1910/30 machine guns during the Second World War.

Heavy Machine Gun

The most powerful machine gun in the Red Army arsenal during the Second World War was the DShK 1938. Red Army personnel nicknamed it the *Dushka*, which translates from the Russian language to 'Sweetheart'. Approximately 8,000 examples of the heavy machine gun (HMG) entered service during the war years.

The DShK 1938 fired a 12.7×108mm rimless round at a rate of fire of about 600 rounds per minute. The weapon resided in the anti-aircraft companies of Red Army infantry divisions. The DShK 1938 also became the main armament of the T-40 light tank and a turret roof-mounted anti-aircraft gun for late-war Red Army tanks and self-propelled guns.

The belt-fed air-cooled DShK 1938 weighed about 78lb. The machine-gun's carriage had two configurations: one for engaging ground targets and one for aerial targets. Its three pole-like trails came together for the ground role and attached to a two-wheeled carriage provided with an armoured shield.

When configured for the anti-aircraft role, the two-wheeled carriage and gun shield of the DShK 1938 typically came off and the three trails extended to form a 5ft tripod with 360 degrees of traverse.

Anti-Tank Rifles

For its infantry units the Red Army adopted a single shot anti-tank rifle in October 1939 designated the PTR M1939. The weapon was chambered to fire a new rimless 14.5×114mm (.57 calibre) round. However, an unfounded belief that German tanks had thicker armour than they really had led to the immediate cancellation of the PTR M1939 with only a small number completed.

When the Germans invaded the Soviet Union in June 1941, the Red Army realized that their tanks were thinly-armoured and vulnerable to their 14.5mm anti-tank rifles. This led the Red Army to want as many anti-tank rifles as it could get its hands on as quickly as possible.

As the Red Army felt that the PTR M1939 was too complex and costly to build in large numbers, an emergency programme resulted in the manufacture of the single-shot bolt-action PTRD-41 and the semi-automatic PTRS-41.

About 18,000 examples of the single-shot PTRD-41 came down the assembly lines by the end of 1941 and almost 185,000 the following year. The production of the semi-automatic PTRS-41 anti-tank gun never matched that of its single-shot counterpart. Only 77 examples of the PTRS-41 came off the factory floor in 1941, and a more impressive total of about 63,000 the following year. Both weapons would serve until the end of the Second World War.

The PTRD-41 had a length of 79.5in and a weight of about 38lb. At 84in long, the PTRS-41 weighed 46lb. The 14.5mm rounds they fired could effectively penetrate the armour on German light and medium tanks in 1941. From a translated Red Army report found on the Tank Archives Blog comparing the PTRD-41 and the PTRS-41 comes the following:

> Almost all anti-tank rifle units speak well of the PTRD: light to carry and flawless in battle. Some wish to increase its rate of fire; others mention that the rate of fire is the only good quality of the PTRS. There are no positive reviews of its reliability, only negative.

The frontal armour array of up-armoured German medium tanks fielded in 1942 and early 1943 proved immune to the Red Army's anti-tank guns. However, the tanks remained vulnerable on their sides and rear to the 14.5mm round till the end of the war. In the November 1942 American military publication *Intelligence Bulletin* comes the following translated passage from a Red Army source:

> In destroying German tanks, Russian anti-tank riflemen follow a set of directions, which are given here in condensed form as a matter of information:
>
> 1. Show daring. Let the enemy tanks come within 200 yards or closer. The best range is 100 to 200 yards. Don't let the enemy fire lead you to open your own fire too soon.
> 2. The anti-tank rifle can fire 8 to 10 rounds per minute, if the gunner and his assistant use teamwork. The gunner opens and closes the breech, aims and fires; the assistant, lying on his right, cleans and oils the shell and places it in the chamber.
> 3. Remember that for a distance of as much as 400 yards, the effect of the wind need not be considered.
> 4. Remember the deflection correction for the movement of the tank. At a speed of 22.5 miles per hour, a lead of 1 yard is required for every 100 yards of range.
> 5. Aim for the rear of the turret – the gunner and ammunition are there. If you hit the ammunition, you can blow up the tank.
> 6. Fire at the center of the rear half of the tank – the motor and the fuel containers are there. If you hit either one, you will put the tank out of action.
> 7. A well-camouflaged gun crew can put any tank out of action with well-aimed shots, and can block a road to a whole column of tanks.

The following information about the tactical employment of Russian anti tank rifles appeared in *Red Star*, an official Soviet wartime publication:

> The greatest success has been attained by squads consisting of two or three anti-tank rifles placed 15 to 20 yards apart. Such units can bring effective fire to bear on a target and have a greater chance of putting it out of commission than fire by a single rifle would have.

A Desperate Measure

In the frantic days of the summer of 1941 when it seemed that nothing could stop the advance of the tank-led German armies into the Soviet Union, the lack of sufficient infantry anti-tank weapons led to Soviet factory production of standardized gasoline (petrol) bombs, best known today by their wartime Finnish Army nickname of 'Molotov Cocktails'. In the Red Army they were referred to as 'bottles with flammable mixture'. These supplemented the improvised incendiary versions made by Red Army soldiers in the field.

In selecting positions for anti-tank titles [*sic*], detailed reconnaissance of the target area should be made, in addition to the usual local reconnaissance. Eliminating dead spots and protecting against the most likely routes of enemy tank approach are important considerations. The positions should be echeloned so as to be mutually supporting with fire from the flanks.

In fortifying these positions, it has proved impracticable to construct emplacements with roofs because of increased visibility to the enemy air force and lack of 360° traverse. The best types of emplacements are open and circular in shape, with a diameter large enough to permit free movement of the crew for all-around traverse and to protect the gun and crew from being crushed by enemy tanks.

In the preparation of anti-tank fire, the rifleman should select five or six key reference points at different ranges, measure the distance to them, and study the intervening terrain. When actually firing, he should fire at stationary tanks whenever possible and not take leads at ranges over 400 yards. Aim should always be taken at the vulnerable parts, taking advantage of any hesitation or exposure of the sides of the enemy tanks.

Infantry Guns

As with most large armies of its day, the Red Army subdivided its towed artillery pieces into categories. The smallest artillery pieces fell within the general English language classification of infantry guns. Such weapons had to be sufficiently small and light to be moved around the battlefield with muscle power.

The Red Army, in 1928, introduced into field service the 76mm Regimental Gun M1927. It had an interrupted screw breech mechanism. Muzzle velocity came in at 1,270ft/s when firing a 14lb high-explosive (HE) round to a maximum range of around 2.6 miles. The weapon's rate of fire with a trained crew was between ten and twelve rounds per minute. Soviet industry completed approximately 18,000 examples of the M1927 by 1943.

In a passage from the book titled *Panzer Killers: Anti-Tank Warfare on the Eastern Front*, a Red Army soldier who served as a crewman on an M1927 recalled:

Over the entire Winter War [30 November 1939 to 13 March 1940], we perhaps fired several times from defilade positions, since we spent nearly all

Artillery Breech Mechanism

An interrupted screw breech mechanism consists of a threaded chamber at the breech end of the barrel and a mating threaded plug; in essence, the plug screws into the threaded chamber at the breech end of the barrel. However, sections of threading are missing – 'interrupted' – from complementary areas inside the breech and on the plug, so as the plug is inserted into the breech, threaded sections along the plug slide into empty channels in the breech. Then the plug is turned as little as one-eighth of a turn to mate the threads and seal the breech.

The advantages of interrupted screw breech mechanisms include their strength, reducing weight in the cannon's breech section and uniform distribution of longitudinal stresses generated by the gas pressure developed in firing, along with shortening the time the gunners need to lock the breech.

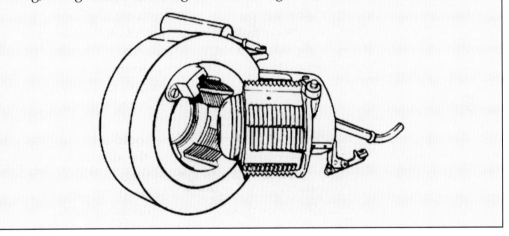

our time manhandling the guns forward behind the advancing infantry, always firing over open sights. We'd take a ridgeline, advance 100 to 200 metres [109 to 219 yards], and then make no headway for about a week. We'd then make another 100 to 200 metres advance and again come to a grinding halt. That's how we broke through the [Finnish Army] Mannerheim Line.

The Red Army's displeasure with the gun's original box trail towed carriage led Soviet industry to fit the gun onto the more modern carriage of the 45mm Anti-Tank Gun M1942 (M-42). The new combination became the 76mm Regimental Gun M1943. It weighed 1,332lb. Production of the Model 1943 concluded in 1945 with around 4,000 examples built.

Light Mortars

During the Second World War, the Red Army divided its mortars between light, medium and heavy classifications. The smallest was the 37mm Spade Mortar that initially saw use during the First Russo-Finnish War, lasting in service until the

German invasion. Its replacement, a series of progressively improved 50mm mortars, culminated in the 50mm PM 40. Industry completed 174,868 examples of the 50mm mortars.

The 50mm mortars weighed around 20lb and fired 1.9lb HE rounds to a maximum range of 440 yards. As long as there was sufficient ammunition, the crew could fire up to thirty rounds per minute. From a translated Red Army report dated 29 May 1945 found on the Tank Archives blog is the following passage on the 50mm mortar:

> In order for the division to independently complete tactical objectives, its artillery must be reinforced. The 50mm mortars used by rifle companies have shown themselves useless while penetrating enemy defenses and during pursuit. In defensive battles, when both sides have constructed trenches at full depth, the 50mm mortar is not very effective at ranges from 300 to 1,000 meters [328 to 1,094 yards]. When these mortars fire, the enemy usually detects them and responds with massed artillery fire, which causes disproportionate losses. The 50mm mortar has little impact in offensive or defensive battles and should be removed from use.

Medium Mortar

The Red Army classified its 82mm mortars as medium mortars. Like its 50mm counterpart, the larger mortar appeared in a series of progressively improved versions, with the final model designated the 82mm Model 1943 (82-PM43). In total Soviet industry built 167,281 examples of the 82mm mortar between 1937 and 1944. The 82mm mortar weighed approximately 140lb and fired 7.5lb HE rounds out to a range of almost 2 miles.

To aid the mortar crews in moving the weapon around the battlefield, two small metal wheels were attached to its base plate. These came off before firing on early-production examples. In later-production examples, the wheels pivoted upward before firing. A mortar base plate provides a firm base from which a mortar is fired and allows the mortar's employment on soft or hard ground.

Mortar Fans

In the book titled *The Encyclopedia of Infantry Weapons of World War Two* by weapons expert Ian V. Hogg is the following passage on the Red Army's favourable view of mortars in all sizes:

> Generally speaking, the Russians were the greatest mortar enthusiasts, and this, of course, comes back to their great love of keeping things simple. Mortars are cheap and easy to make; their ammunition is cheap and less difficult to manufacture than normal artillery ammunition. They are easy to operate, and for their caliber, they deliver a much larger load of explosives on the enemy than a gun ... To use the modern jargon, the cost-effectiveness of the mortar is high.

The Red Army also formed motorcycle units equipped with the 82mm mortar, an arrangement never duplicated by other armies. The mortar and its base plate resided on the motorcycle's sidecar. When halted, the two-man crew removed it from the sidecar and erected it on the ground before firing. The advantage of the arrangement was that the two-man crew could quickly drive away after a fire mission before enemy counter-battery fire could take effect.

In the May 1946 issue of the American-published *Intelligence Bulletin* there appears an article titled 'On the Way: The Employment of Mortars in the Red Army':

> Each battalion 82mm Mortar Company, with nine pieces, may fire in support of its own rifle battalion. It is normal practice, however, when on the defense or in a static situation, to combine the three medium mortar companies of a rifle regiment into a provisional battalion commanded by the regimental heavy mortar [120mm] battery commander, whose pieces operate jointly with those of the three mortar companies. This provisional mortar battalion establishes a fire direction center with wire communication to observation posts and to platoons through their company command posts … The provisional battalion commander is in turn under the command and coordination of the division artillery headquarters … Thus, the provisional medium mortar battalion … may fire massed concentrations in support of the entire regimental front, or may on occasion fire into the sectors of adjacent regiments, range permitting.

Heavy Mortars

At the upper end of the scale of mortars, the Red Army fielded two heavy infantry support mortar examples. The first, the 107mm GVPM-38 mortar or M1938, was intended for use by specialized mountain units. The mortar weighed 370lb and broke down into smaller pieces for transportation.

The 107mm mortar could also be towed into action by a horse team or a wheeled vehicle. It fired 20lb HE rounds out to a range of around 4 miles, with the crew able to fire fifteen rounds per minute. Soviet industry only built 1,574 examples of the 107mm mortars.

The second heavy mortar employed by the Red Army, the 120mm PM-38 or M1938, weighed 1,052lb with its two-wheeled carriage and fired 35lb rounds up to 4 miles. The rate of fire topped out at about ten rounds per minute. Soviet industry completed 49,981 examples of the mortar between 1940 and 1944.

A 1946 War Department publication lists the roles performed by the Red Army 120mm M1938 heavy mortar:

> Primary missions of the [120mm] mortar brigade includes destruction of personnel in the open and in light shelters; destruction of light field fortifications and wire barriers; destruction or neutralization of artillery, mortar and infantry firing positions; accompanying and defensive barrages and concentrations; and smoke screens.

> **Mortar Facts**
>
> Mortar rounds are semi-fixed since part of their propellant charge may be removed to vary their range. They also have stabilizing fins since they were fired from smooth-bore barrels. The standard method of adjusting mortar fire is by bracketing the target for range.
>
> No two mortar rounds have the same trajectory or explode at the same point, despite being fired one after the other, just like artillery shells. The reasons include the need to leave a gap to allow the round to slide down the barrel, air density, temperature and wind.

Like the 107mm M1938, the 120mm M1938 broke down into separate pieces for transportation, including a two-wheeled carriage. The preferred method of moving the weapon was a horse team or a wheeled vehicle. The German Army thought so highly of the Red Army's 120mm mortar that they employed captured examples and began building a copy.

A German officer noted in a report of a March 1942 battle that the Red Army combined its 120mm mortar fire with fire from conventional artillery pieces:

> Occasionally, the Russians added artillery fire to the fire of their mortars when shelling combat installations on the German main line of resistance and the German battle positions. The results of this double fire steadily became more and more effective. In the Petukhovka sector and at Vesniny, the German artillery observers one day noticed the fire coordination with respect to timing and areas of the fire of Russian 80mm [*sic* 82mm] and 120mm [*sic*] mortars and Russian artillery, particularly in the preparation of Russian advances … Scrupulous observation disclosed that the Russians first adjusted the fire of their mortars on a target and then doubled up the initial fire for effect from their mortars with artillery fire, which, as a result, was well-placed from the outset. The Russian artillery itself, however, was located so far to the rear that it was able to reach the German battle position only by means of long-range fire.

Grenades

As with all Second World War armies, the Red Army provided its infantrymen with hand grenades, the most numerous of which were the fragmentation type with a four- to five-second fusing delay.

The Red Army's hand grenades came in several configurations, including a stick grenade, a rounded example with a serrated body nicknamed the 'Lemon' by Red Army personnel and a cylinder-shaped model. In addition, there were two anti-tank grenades. The initial anti-tank version bore the designation RPG-40 and had an HE warhead. An improved model bearing the title RPG-43 came with a shaped-charge warhead (hollow charge). Both anti-tank grenades weighed about 3lb and were fitted with impact fuses.

Mines

Like other armies, the Red Army fielded a range of pressure-activated anti-personnel and anti-tank mines. In *Russian Combat Methods in World War Two* is the following passage on their employment in the defensive role:

> The Russians made extensive use of mines. As a rule, a protective mine belt was to be found about 8 to 10 yards in front of the most forward trench. Terrain particularly favorable for an enemy approach likewise was heavily mined. The Russians preferred to employ wooden box mines, which could not be detected by the standard mine-detectors. In the depth of the battle position, mines were laid in unexpected places. In favorable terrain, anti-tank mines were numerous.

From a US Army manual dated May 1948 and titled 'Land Mine Warfare' is the following passage on Red Army/Soviet Army employment of mines in offensive operations:

> In the Russian Army, engineer parties are attached directly to infantry assault units. Each engineer soldier carries two or three mines which are employed at any point where the attack slows down or where an enemy counterattack develops. This includes mining the flanks of advancing units and units in salient positions. This tactic protects infantry units from being overrun or cut off by armor-supported counterattacks.

Weapon Failures

Somebody in the Red Army came up with the bold idea in the 1930s of strapping explosives to medium-sized dogs fitted with an upright pressure-activated wooden lever. The idea was to feed the selected dogs only under Red Army tanks' hulls and acclimatize them to tank noises so that when released on the battlefield, the Red Army anticipated that they would seek out German tanks and blow themselves up as they sought food under the enemy tanks.

In practice, the idea of dog mines soon showed itself badly flawed as the animals tended to seek more familiar Red Army tanks in the process of looking for food. Another problem encountered on the battlefield was that the less bold dogs became frightened by battlefield noises and sought out their handlers for comfort. They had to shoot them before returning lest they should accidentally detonate in the handler's presence.

Supposedly a small number of German tanks were destroyed or damaged by the dog mines. The Red Army claimed their dog mines destroyed up to 300 German tanks. In *Russian Combat Methods in World War Two* written by former German officers is the following passage on dog mines:

> New of this insidious improvisation caused some alarm in the German panzer units and made them fire at all approaching dogs on sight. So far, there is no evidence of any case where a German tank was destroyed by a

dog mine. On the other hand, it was reported that several mine dogs fleeing from the fire of German tanks sought protection underneath Russian tanks, which promptly blew up. One thing is certain: the spectre of the mine dogs ceased just as abruptly as it had begun.

The seven-shot Nagant M1895 revolver weighed 1.8lb and had a length of 10.5in. It came in both single- and double-action configurations. With its fixed cylinder, which allowed reloading only one round at a time, the weapon proved time-consuming to empty and reload. Modern writers on small arms note the stiff trigger pull of the double-action model. *(Dreamstime)*

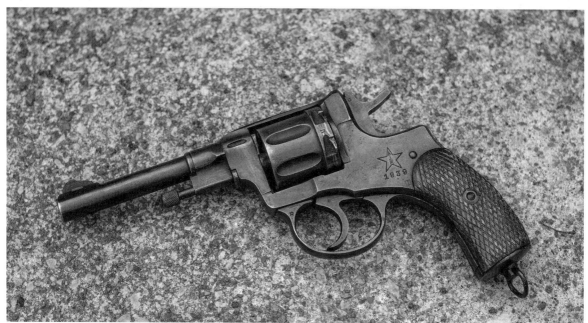

The replacement for the Nagant 1895 revolver appeared in the 1930s as a semi-automatic pistol nicknamed the 'Tokarev' after its designer Fedor Tokarev. He borrowed most of the weapon's design features from the American Colt M1911 automatic pistol. The Tokarev had an eight-round magazine and came in two models: the TT-31 and the improved TT-33 pictured here. The weapon weighed 1.88lb and had a length of 7.6in. (*Dreamstime*)

A Russian re-enactor dressed in a reproduction Second World War Red Army uniform fires his bayonet-equipped Mosin-Nagant M1891/30 bolt-action rifle. For most Red Army infantrymen from rural backgrounds, their rifles proved to be the most complex piece of machinery they had ever encountered. Due to wartime shortages, rubberized canvas ammunition pouches replaced the original leather-made examples. (*Dreamstime*)

The Mosin-Nagant M1891/30 bolt-action rifle pictured here in the hands of a Russian re-enactor has a five-round integral magazine loaded with a charger. As the rifle has an interrupter, you can top off the weapon's magazine with single rounds if required. The rifle's length, not counting its normally attached 17in bayonet, is 48.5in. It weighs in at 8.8lb. Despite its age, the weapon was rather popular with Red Army soldiers due to its reliability under the harshest conditions. (*Dreamstime*)

Batches of Mosin-Nagant M1891/30 bolt-action rifles came off the production lines for converting into sniper rifles, as seen here in the hands of Red Army sniper Lieutenant Ziba Ganiyeva. Note the turn-down bolt handle, a design feature of sniper rifles. The weapon has the 4-power scope designated the PEM (Unified Model Improved) that began appearing in 1936. (*Author's collection*)

A model in a reproduction Red Army uniform poses with a Mosin-Nagant M1891/30 bolt-action sniper rifle. The rifle has a 3.5-power PU scope initially intended for a semi-automatic sniper rifle. Hence it was offset to the right to allow for loading and the ejection of spent rounds from the gun's ejection port in the receiver. (*Dreamstime*)

The 48.5in length of the Mosin-Nagant M1891/30 bolt-action rifle made it awkward for Red Army soldiers operating crew-served weapons. To provide them with a gun better suited to their needs, Soviet industry came up with two shorter carbines with a length of approximately 40in. The older of the two, designated the M1938, weighed 7.5lb. The more modern carbine was designated the M1944 as pictured here, weighed 9lb and came with a folding bayonet. (*Dreamstime*)

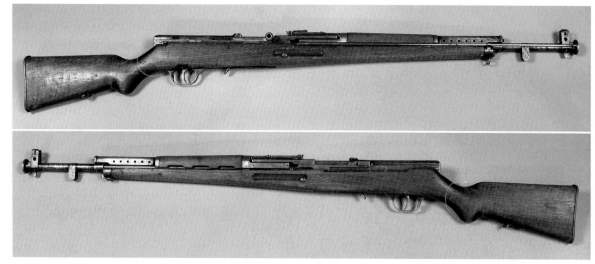

(**Above**) In 1937 the Red Army fielded the semi-automatic AVS-36 rifle pictured here. Its designer was Sergei Simonov, who had begun work on the weapon in 1930. The AVS-36 had a length of 48.4in and weighed 9.5lb. It came with a fifteen-round magazine (not seen here). Unfortunately the weapon had some unresolved design issues that caused the Red Army to halt its production in 1940. (*Swedish Army Museum*)

(**Below**) An overlapping series of semi-automatic rifle designs which the Red Army ordered into production in 1939 included the Fedor Tokarev-designed SVT-38 semi-automatic rifle. The weapon weighed 8.5lb and had a length of 48.3in not including its bayonet. It, however, also proved to have some early design issues that led to production of this pictured improved model designated the SVT-40 beginning in June 1940. (*Dreamstime*)

(**Opposite, above**) Pictured here are Red Army soldiers with some captured enemy forces. The Soviet infantryman on the left holds an SVT-40, which weighed 8.5lb and had a length minus the bayonet of 48.3in. In comparison, the semi-automatic American M1 Garand, without its bayonet, weighed approximately 9lb and had a length of only 43in. (*Author's collection*)

(**Opposite, below**) A Russian re-enactor poses with an SVT-40 semi-automatic rifle. The Red Army had initially envisioned that the SVT-40 would eventually replace all its bolt-action Mosin-Nagant M1891/30 rifles. However, the German invasion ended that plan as the Red Army lost hundreds of thousands of their SVT-40s early on. The Red Army was therefore forced to ramp up production of M1891/30 rifles and cheap, straightforward submachine guns. (*Dreamstime*)

(**Above**) The Red Army soldier in the foreground holds a PPD-40 submachine gun. It weighed about 8lb without its drum magazine and had a length of 31in. Its designer, Vasily A. Degtyaryov, based it on the German post-First World War MP-28/II submachine gun. His original version of the submachine gun, the PPD-34, evolved into the improved PPD-34/38 model, which led to the less complicated PPD-40. (*Author's collection*)

(**Below**) Wanting an even less complex and hence cheaper and faster to build submachine gun than the PPD-40, Soviet industry placed into production the PPSh-41 pictured here and designed by Georgy Shpagin. Like the PPD-40, it came with a seventy-one-round drum magazine copied from a Finnish design. The PPSh-41 was about 2in longer than the PDD-40. (*Dreamstime*)

(**Opposite, above**) A German soldier is shown here surrendering to a Red Army opponent armed with a PPSh-41. During the weapon's production run, it appeared with two different types of sights. The early-production PPSh-41s had a fixed rear tangent sight. Later-production examples came with a flip-type aperture sight. In close-quarter engagements, users aimed their weapons based on observing the fall of the shots and then adjusting their fire. (*Author's collection*)

(**Below**) A re-enactor dressed as a Red Army soldier of the Second World War is seen here posing with a PPSh-41. The weapon's wartime manual stressed that before firing, soldiers needed to adopt a stable posture quickly and lean into the submachine gun to counteract its recoil. Due to the PPSh-41's high rate of fire and ammunition consumption, it became the job of non-commissioned officers (NCOs) and junior officers to monitor the firing rate of men under their command. (*Dreamstime*)

Shown together here are a PPSh-41 with its Finnish-inspired seventy-one-round drum magazine and thirty-five-round box magazine, and a PPS-43 with its thirty-five-round box magazine. The magazines were not interchangeable between the two weapons. The PPS-43 was designed by Alexei I. Sudarev and weighed about 7lb. Even simpler in design than the PPSh-41, it consisted of almost all stamped steel parts spot-welded together; the only machined parts were the barrel and bolt. The PPS-42 not pictured was the earlier version of what became the PPS-43. (*Dreamstime*)

Among the many weapons that Vasily A. Degtyaryov designed for the Red Army was the air-cooled DP light machine gun pictured here. Its most defining external feature was its horizontal forty-seven-round pan magazine required due to the rimmed 7×54mmR cartridge used. Degtyaryov had begun work on its design in 1921, with the Red Army accepting the weapon into service in 1928. It had a length of about 51in and weighed around 25lb loaded. (*Dreamstime*)

The Degtyaryov DP light machine gun's horizontal pan magazine shown here proved to be a weak spot in the weapon's design. It proved fragile in field use if handled roughly. As with the drum magazines of the Red Army's submachine guns, loading the DP's horizontal pan magazine proved time-consuming and difficult. When advancing, the weapon was light enough to fire from the hip or an underarm position. (*Author's collection*)

A Degtyaryov DP light machine gun is seen here on a Red Army motorcycle's sidecar. Wartime-built Soviet motorcycles and sidecars were copies of a German prewar design. Under Lend-Lease the Red Army received from the United States about 26,000 Harley-Davidson solo motorcycles. The Red Army would add sidecars to them. The British government also provided the Red Army with motorcycles from many firms, including Norton, Matchless and BSA. (*Author's collection*)

Such was the demand for Degtyaryov DP light machine guns that the model intended for tanks designated the DT was pressed into service as an infantry weapon. Instead of the standard wooden stock, the DT version had a telescopic metal stock and a folding metal bipod, as seen in this wartime photograph. Instead of the horizontal forty-seven-round pan magazine, it retained the sixty-round horizontal pan magazine intended for tanks as well as a thicker barrel. (*Author's collection*)

Degtyaryov began work on a new light machine gun design in 1934, accepted by the Red Army in 1944 as the RPD, with an example pictured here. Instead of the standard 7×54mmR round used in the DP, the RPD fired a new 7.62×39mm rimless intermediate round. It weighed only 16lb without its 100-round drum magazine inserted. Not wanting to interrupt production of the DP, the RPD did not enter Soviet Army service (the successor to the Red Army) in large numbers until 1953. (*Dreamstime*)

These Red Army re-enactors are posing with a water-cooled Model 1910/30 medium machine gun. They are wearing the wartime SSh-40 helmet. The designer of the machine gun was American-born Hiram Maxim, who demonstrated his initial prototype of the weapon in 1884. It proved to be the world's first fully automatic machine gun. Production of a modified version of the weapon for the Imperial Russian Army began in 1910. (*Dreamstime*)

In reproduction Second World War Red Army uniforms, re-enactors pull a water-cooled Maxim Model 1910/30 medium machine gun during a living history demonstration. The weapon had a rate of fire between 520 to 580rpm and an effective range of around 1,000 yards. Including the two-wheeled cart with its armoured shield, the weapon weighed about 150lb. It fired the same 7.62 × 54mmR round as the Mosin-Nagant 1891/30 rifle. (*Dreamstime*)

Well aware of the limitations of the water-cooled Model 1910/30 medium machine gun due to its weight and size, the Red Army sought a suitable replacement. Designer Peter M. Goryunov came up with the answer: the air-cooled SG-43 medium machine gun. The weapon and its two-wheeled carriage pictured here weighed about 90lb. It fired the 7.62 × 54mmR cartridge at 500 to 700rpm. This particular example was postwar-built, as is evident from its fluted barrel. (*Dreamstime*)

Intended to be employed against both ground and aerial targets, the air-cooled DShK heavy machine gun is seen here in its anti-aircraft configuration. Adopted by the Red Army in 1938, the machine gun and its two-wheeled carriage came in at around 346lb. It fired a powerful 12.7 × 108mm round at about 600rpm. The weapon incorporated design features by both Vasily Degtyaryov and George Shpagin. The latter was the designer of the PPSh-41 submachine gun. (*Author's collection*)

In 1938 the Red Army began looking at adopting a 14.5mm anti-tank rifle. However, nothing much came of it as the only submission proved overly complex and not as reliable as hoped. When the Germans invaded, the call went out for a simpler and more cost-effective anti-tank rifle. Both Vasily A. Degtyaryov and Sergei G. Simonov responded. The former came up with the single-shot example pictured here and referred to as the PTRD-41. (*Author's collection*)

A five-round example of the semi-automatic PTRS-41 designed by Sergei G. Simonov is visible in this wartime photograph. It proved both heavier and longer than Degtyaryov's PTRD-41 and far less reliable. The problem came from fouling (residues) generated by the 14.5×108mm rounds it fired, which often jammed the weapon's gas-operated mechanism. As both anti-tank rifles had only iron sights, engagement range hovered at around 1,000 yards. (*Author's collection*)

Pictured here is an example of the Soviet factory-made wooden crate intended to deliver standardized gasoline (incendiary) bombs to Red Army infantry units. The term 'Molotov Cocktail' was a sarcastic Finnish Army nickname for their own improvised and factory-made gasoline bombs named after the Soviet foreign minister Vyacheslav Molotov. (*Author's collection*)

In 1935 the Red Army took into service its first man-portable flame-thrower designated the ROKS-2, followed by the simplified ROKS-3. A captured example of the latter is seen here with a Finnish soldier. Note that the builder made the flame-gun portion of the weapon vaguely resemble an 1890/30 Mosin-Nagant rifle, the reason being to disguise the weapon and prevent those assigned to carry it from being singled out by the enemy.
(*Public domain*)

(**Opposite, above**) Pictured is a Red Army 76.2mm Regimental Gun M1937. The initial examples had wood-spoked wheels with metal rims suitable for towing by horse teams. With the advent of self-propelled prime movers, the 1,720lb weapon appeared with solid rubber tyres. Later the gun went onto a lighter weight 45mm anti-tank gun carriage, resulting in its new designation as the 76.2mm Regimental Gun M1943. (*Dreamstime*)

(**Above**) A Red Army soldier firing a 50mm mortar. The initial model bore the designation PM-38 or M1938. Following was a succession of simplified and improved versions, with the final model labelled the M1941. All fired a 1.5lb HE round to a maximum distance of 900 yards. The 50mm mortar proved unpopular due to its small explosive content, with Red Army soldiers preferring the larger 82mm mortars. (*Author's collection*)

(**Opposite, below**) As with 50mm mortars, the Red Army went through a progressively-improved series of 82mm mortars, with a wartime example pictured here. The first model received the designation of the PM-36 and the final model became the PM-43. The combination of mortar tube, bipod and two-wheeled base plate weighed in at around 130lb. With the wheels removed, the 82mm mortars weighed about 100lb. The 82mm mortar fired roughly 7lb HE rounds to a maximum range of 2 miles. (*Author's collection*)

Pictured here is a Red Army 120mm mortar labelled 120mm PM-38 or M1938 in action. Note the size of the 35lb mortar rounds which it could fire to a maximum range of approximately 4 miles, with a well-trained crew able to fire ten rounds per minute. Most mortar rounds are streamlined and tapered at the rear to a tail boom with attached stabilizing fins. Other terms for mortar rounds are 'bombs' or 'shells'. (*Author's collection*)

Shown here in its travelling configuration is a Red Army 120mm mortar. When towed, the mortar weighed in at around 1,000lb, and when set up for firing its weight dropped to about 600lb following removal of its transport carriage. The mortar's base plate, visible in this image, consists of a large pressed steel body that provides stability, preserving the lay (aim) of the weapon when fired. The rear of the mortar tube fits into a central socket in the base plate, held in place by a locking lever. (*Dreamstime*)

The Red Army infantryman pictured here is ready for anything, with four fragmentation grenades stuffed into a belt alongside a bayonet. He is wearing the SSh-40 steel helmet, the most common model used during the Second World War. Surprisingly, many Red Army soldiers believed that wearing a helmet was cowardly or was too restricting to wear. The soldier shown is also wearing the standard-issue shelter cape. (*Author's collection*)

Chapter Two

Light Tanks

The Russian Imperial Army did not field any tanks during the First World War (1914–18). After the Tsar's fall in the spring of 1917 and the resultant rise to power of the Bolsheviks under Vladimir Lenin, anti-Bolshevik forces aligned with the former Tsarist regimes received military equipment, including tanks, from the British and French governments.

One of the Western Allies' tanks provided to the anti-Bolshevik forces was the two-man, French-designed and built Renault FT light tank that first saw combat in France against the German Army in 1918. Armament consisted of either a turret-mounted 8mm machine gun or a short-barrelled low-velocity 37mm gun. The gasoline-engine-powered vehicle weighed 8 tons and had a maximum armour thickness on the turret front of 22mm.

During the Russian Civil War (1917–24) between the Bolsheviks and anti-Bolshevik forces referred to as the 'Whites', a small number of Renaults fell into the hands of the Red Army created in June 1918.

To build up their tank strength during the civil war, the Red Army decided to reverse-engineer the Renault. By August 1920, the first example came off the factory floor. After three months of testing, the vehicle received the name of the 'Freedom Fighter Lenin' tank.

The Red Army had fourteen additional examples of the reversed-engineered Renault built between 1921 and 1922. However, none ever saw combat. Power for the Red Army versions of the Renault came from Italian-designed and built gasoline-powered engines.

MS-1 Light Tank

The Soviet Union, created in December 1922, decided to undertake a massive policy of industrialization during the 1920s and early 1930s, resulting in the purchase of large amounts of foreign-made industrial machinery. Much of that came from the United States between 1929 and 1932. That machinery provided the Soviet Union with the ability to build various vehicles, both wheeled and tracked. The American Ford Motor Company played a leading role in helping Soviet industry build the necessary factories.

The first tank to roll out of a Soviet factory in 1928 was the gasoline-engine-powered two-man MS-1 light tank (also known as the T-18). Derived from the French Renault FT of First World War fame, it appeared with a Soviet-designed suspension system intended to improve off-road performance. Production of the MS-1 began in 1928 and continued until 1931, with 959 examples completed.

The MS-1 initially mounted a slightly improved version of the original French-designed and built 37mm gun fitted to the Renault FT. Instead of a coaxial machine gun, it had two 7.62mm machine guns in a separate mount on the turret's right-hand side. The 7-ton tank first saw combat during the Sino-Soviet conflict of 1929.

The building of the MS-1 in relatively large numbers by Soviet industry proved to be an impressive achievement. This was especially true for a country that had just transitioned from a primarily agricultural-based economy.

There existed a plan to modernize the MS-1 with a new gasoline-powered engine and a longer-barrelled 37mm main gun, but that programme came to an end due to rising costs. Only one example came out of the factory doors.

When the MS-1s reached the end of their service lives, some of their turrets were retained as pillboxes along the country's borders. A number had their original French 37mm guns replaced with a 45mm gun.

T-27 Tankette

Due to a shortage of engineering talent in the Soviet Union, no wholly indigenous tank designs of this period were acceptable to the Red Army. It therefore depended on foreign-designed armoured vehicles for inspiration. One of these proved to be the two-man Carden-Loyd Mark VI, built and marketed by British firm Vickers-Armstrong. Each crew member of the Carden-Loyd Mark VI vehicle had an overhead armoured cover.

By today's standards, the almost 2-ton Carden-Loyd Mark VI fell within the light tank category. However, the term 'tankette' was popular during the inter-war period among many armies when describing these small turretless vehicles fitted with forward-firing machine guns.

The Red Army decided in early 1931, after extensive testing of twenty-six examples in the Soviet Union, that the Carden-Loyd Mark VI was suitable for the infantry support and reconnaissance roles. That decision resulted in an order for approximately 5,000 licensed but modified examples designated the T-27, with production beginning in 1931. A progressively improved version became the T-27A.

Like the original British vehicle, the Red Army T-27 series had a two-man crew sitting side by side, armed with a single forward-firing machine gun. Frontal armour protection topped out at 10mm. At one point, the Red Army had considered arming the T-27 series with a 37mm gun, but that never occurred. The Red Army's tankettes received power from a licence-built copy of an American Ford Motor Company gasoline-powered truck engine.

Service use soon demonstrated to the Red Army that the T-27 series had little to offer due to its poor off-road mobility and the lack of a weapon-armed turret which hindered its battlefield usefulness. Therefore the Red Army ordered production halted in 1933 with a total of 3,328 examples completed.

Other than aiding the Red Army in suppressing a guerrilla movement in Soviet Central Asia that ended in 1934, the T-27 series saw no further combat. At one point in the 1930s, the Red Army experimented with the concept of attaching a single T-27 to the bottom fuselage of large multi-engine bombers for delivery to airports captured by Red Army parachutists. However, the idea never progressed past the testing stage.

When the Germans invaded the Soviet Union in June 1941 (Operation BARBAROSSA) the Red Army had already relegated its T-27 series tankettes to secondary roles. These included use as training vehicles or repurposed as prime movers for towing small anti-tank guns.

T-37A Amphibious Light Tank

The Red Army also acquired eight examples of a British-designed and built Vickers-Armstrongs' two-man amphibious tank armed with a turret-mounted machine gun. The idea of such a vehicle caught the imagination of some Red Army officers as they considered the country's undeveloped road infrastructure and many waterways.

The Red Army's plans called for the British amphibious tank to act as a starting-point to develop their own version intended to replace the T-27 series in the reconnaissance role. The model eventually chosen became the T-37 and weighed in at 3.5 tons. An improved model became the T-37A.

The two-man T-37 amphibious series tanks rode on a suspension system derived from a French design. They received power from the same American Ford Motor Company-designed gasoline-powered truck engine found in the T-27 series. Maximum armour thickness topped out at 9mm. A total of 1,954 examples came off the assembly lines between 1933 and 1936.

A total of seventy-five examples of the T-37 featured a flame-thrower instead of the standard 7.62mm machine gun. These received the prefix letters 'KhT', indicating a chemical tank.

Some 673 examples of the T-37 series came with radios and were classified as command vehicles. They were assigned the designation T-37RT, the suffix 'RT' standing for radio tank, and featured a metal frame antenna mounted on the hull's top that encircled the vehicle's superstructure and turret.

Building a sufficient number of suitable radios for tanks and the rest of the Red Army proved an insurmountable problem for Soviet industry throughout the Second World War. The radios built proved to be inferior to German military radios of the time.

Special-Purpose Variant

An unmanned and unarmed radio-controlled demolition version of the T-37 received the designation T-37TT. When encountering a strong enemy defensive position, a T-37TT was stuffed with explosives.

A radio command tank (referred to as the T-37TU) directed the T-37TT towards the chosen enemy defensive position. Upon reaching the objective, the T-37TT's cargo was detonated by a radio signal to clear an opening for follow-on manned tanks.

T-38 Amphibious Light Tank

An extensively redesigned version of the T-37 series with a broader and lower hull and a new machine gun-armed turret received the designation T-38. Its amphibious capabilities were considered superior to those of its predecessor.

The armament of each of the T-38 series tanks was a single 7.62mm machine gun, although some were up-armed in the field with a 20mm gun. The maximum armour thickness of the T-38 was 9mm. The 7,392lb vehicle was in production between 1936 and 1937, with 1,228 examples constructed. Of those produced, only 165 had radios.

The T-38 would first see combat (along with the T-37) with the Red Army's invasion and occupation of the eastern portion of Poland in September and October 1939. The Red Army would also use them during the First Russo-Finnish War (30 November 1939 to 13 March 1940).

Following the German invasion of the Soviet Union, the T-37A and T-38 tanks' job became infantry support rather than reconnaissance. Some of the Red Army's T-37As and T-38s would survive long enough to take part in their second offensive against Finland that took place between 25 June 1941 and 19 September 1944, referred to as the 'Second Russo-Finnish War' or the 'Continuation War'.

T-40 Amphibious Light Tank

Never stopping for long to improve its tank inventory, the Red Army sought a replacement for the T-38 before the German invasion of 1941. That tank was approved for production in December 1939 as the T-40 amphibious tank.

The two-man T-40 was a gasoline-engine-powered vehicle that weighed 6 tons and was the first Red Army tank to feature torsion bar suspension. Previous Red Army light tanks had employed truck-type leaf-spring or coil-spring suspension. The maximum armour thickness on the front of the T-40's turret was 14mm.

The T-40 had a turret-mounted 12.7mm machine gun and a coaxial 7.62mm machine gun. A total of 221 examples of the vehicle came off Soviet assembly lines before the German invasion.

With a pressing need to produce as many tanks as possible in the shortest period of time, the Red Army decided to make do without the T-40's amphibious features, such as its rear hull propeller. The non-amphibious version of the T-40 received the designation of the T-40S, with 136 of them constructed between July and September 1941 and the suffix 'S' standing for land-operated.

Another non-amphibious version of the T-40 began delivery in August 1941. It featured thicker armour than the original T-40 and eventually appeared with a turret-mounted 20mm gun in place of the 12.7mm machine gun. It retained the 7.62mm coaxial machine gun and received the designation of the T-30, with 335 examples completed between August and October 1941.

T-60 Light Tank

Before the German invasion, the Red Army had yet another two-man light tank design in the works. It was designated the T-60 and was armed with a 20mm gun and a coaxial 7.62mm machine gun. About the same size as the T-40, the gasoline-engine-powered vehicle weighed about 6 tons. The maximum armour protection on the T-60 turret's front was initially 25mm, later increased to 35mm.

The T-60's design, unlike previous light tank designs, was never intended to be amphibious. It had become clear to the Red Army that amphibious vehicle complexity, higher cost and the effort required to build them were drawbacks. Their thin armour and the small-calibre armament dictated by the requirement to keep their weight down to achieve buoyancy made them semi-useless on the battlefield. Red Army tankers nicknamed the T-60 'a brother's grave for two'.

Production of the T-60 began in July 1941, followed by an improved version in 1942 that had a more powerful gasoline-powered engine. Production of the T-60 ended in September 1942 with a total of 6,022 examples completed. Efforts to up-arm the vehicle proved fruitless as the turret could not handle the recoil forces of larger-calibre guns.

T-70 Light Tank

The T-60's intended replacement was the up-armoured 11-ton T-70 light tank. Maximum armour protection on the front of the vehicle's turret came to 60mm, offering protection from German 37mm anti-tank rounds. The two-man vehicle featured a turret-mounted high-velocity 45mm main gun for dealing with enemy tanks, as well as a coaxial 7.62mm machine gun.

As initially designed, the T-70 received power from two separate unsynchronized gasoline-powered truck engines, each engine responsible for one of the tank's tracks. The powertrain arrangement soon showed itself to be a serious mistake, resulting in a quick redesign. The revised powertrain arrangement consisted of the two gasoline-powered engines coupled together in-line and connected to a standard truck transmission and differential.

Including the revised powertrain, the upgraded model of the T-70 featured an improved suspension system, wider tracks and more robust torsion bars. The vehicle received the designation of the T-70M. The suffix letter 'M' meant 'modified'. Production began in March 1942 and continued until October 1943 with 8,226 examples completed.

A redesigned version of the T-70M featuring a two-man turret received the designation T-80. It featured a maximum armour thickness of 45mm on the front of its turret. However, by the time the 13-ton vehicle entered production, it was clear to the Red Army that light tanks had no viable role on the battlefield. Hence production ended after only seventy five examples came down the assembly lines, not counting two prototypes.

T-26 Light Tank

Among the many British-designed and built tanks acquired prewar by the Red Army was the gasoline-engine-powered Vickers-Armstrong 6-ton light tank, sometimes referred to as the 'Mark E'. It had been tested but never adopted by the British Army. The light tank proved a successful export product for Vickers as it was very much state of the art when introduced.

Vickers sold a total of 140 examples of its 6-ton light tank between 1930 and 1938. Of that number fifteen went to the Soviet Union. Other countries purchasing the Vickers tank included China, Bolivia and Poland.

The Red Army Version

Vickers offered the 6-ton tank in different versions and the Soviet Union bought examples of the twin-turreted version. Each one-man turret was armed with a single machine gun. The British-built vehicle weighed about 7 tons and made a favourable impression on the Red Army during testing. Modifying it to meet Soviet requirements, the Red Army ordered a better-armoured version weighing 10 tons. The Red Army envisioned it as an infantry support tank and labelled it the T-26.

In Red Army service, most of the T-26 tanks had an armament of two 7.62mm machine guns. Production took place between 1931 and 1934, with 2,038 examples completed. Of that number, 450 had one of the two turrets armed with a Soviet industry-derived long-barrelled version of a French 37mm gun.

Welding became the preferred method of construction as it was faster and avoided the rivet-spalling problem on early-production T-26s. However, a lack of trained manpower and the machinery needed to manufacture welded armour plates remained a problem, leading to T-26 series tanks with individual tanks constructed of both riveted and welded armour plates.

Variants

There appeared a small number of turretless T-26 tanks with a hydraulically-operated portable bridge to aid in crossing narrow gaps. Its designation was the ST-26, with the prefix letters 'ST' standing for engineer tank.

A radio-equipped command version of the T-26 appeared in small numbers, with a three-sided metal-frame antenna mounted on its upper hull. These also had one of their two turrets armed with a 37mm gun and became the T-26RT.

As with the T-37A, there was an unmanned radio-controlled T-26 tank and a corresponding radio command vehicle. The unmanned radio-controlled T-26 had a flame-thrower operated by radio control from a command tank.

There were several other T-26 series variants built in small numbers. These included an open-topped version fitted with a forward-firing 122mm howitzer; the vehicle was designated as the SU-5-2 with thirty-three of them built.

An improvised model built in a plant in Leningrad consisted of a T-26 chassis armed with a 76mm artillery piece in a forward-firing position protected by a gun shield. It had several designations, including SU-T-26, with an unknown number being constructed.

There also appeared an open-topped unarmed version configured as a prime mover for artillery pieces. It received the designation of the T-26 with the suffix letter 'T' standing for tractor. A total of 197 examples came off the factory floor.

A Different Configuration

In 1932 the Red Army ordered a modified version of the T-26 with a single turret, operated by two men and armed with a long-barrelled high-velocity 45mm main gun and a coaxial 7.62mm machine gun. The tank weighed 11.5 tons. The Red Army referred to the tank as the single-turret T-26 with the original model labelled as the twin-turret T-26.

The twin-turreted T-26 proved to be the most numerous of the T-26 series built, with 5,500 examples completed between 1933 and 1936, far more than the number of tanks constructed for any other army in the 1930s. Unlike the original twin-turret model of the T-26, the single-turret model had a pronounced turret bustle for 45mm ammunition storage.

Like the twin-turreted T-26, a command tank version of the single-turret T-26 appeared, identified by a horseshoe-shaped metal frame antenna surrounding the turret. The frame antenna proved very vulnerable in combat during the Spanish Civil War (17 July 1936 to 1 April 1939), leaving the tank's radio inoperative. The radios themselves also proved too fragile for field use. Vehicle commanders therefore had to rely on flags to communicate with other vehicles; a tricky choice due to battlefield conditions such as smoke and dust that obscured signalling along with enemy fire.

As with many other tanks, the Red Army did not identify the radio-equipped command examples of the T-26 with any unique prefix or suffix letters. Instead they generally referred to them as 'radio tanks' and those without as 'line tanks'.

Later-production examples of the single-turreted T-26 appeared with two additional 7.62mm machine guns, one in the turret's rear bustle in 1935 and another mounted on the turret roof for anti-aircraft protection in 1937, with an improved mount showing up in 1938. A more potent 45mm gun appeared on the single-turreted T-26 beginning in 1935.

There also appeared an unmanned single-turreted radio-controlled T-26 and a corresponding single-turreted radio command vehicle. As with the earlier version of the unmanned radio-controlled demolition tank based on the twin-turreted T-26, a later version had a radio-controlled flame-thrower. They would take part in the Red Army invasion of eastern Poland without seeing action, but did see combat in the First Russo-Finnish War with disappointing results.

Lessons Learned

During the Spanish Civil War the Soviet government sold 281 single-turreted examples of the 45mm gun-armed T-26 series tanks to the Republican side. These proved far superior to the machine gun-armed light tanks and tankettes provided by the German and Italian governments to the Nationalist side.

Some of the T-26 series tanks had Red Army crews. However, the majority depended on local manpower that was unfortunately not mechanically skilled. Combined with the fact that tanks of the time, especially the engines, were not very durable, the T-26 tanks became plagued by reliability problems, an issue compounded by a lack of trained maintenance personnel and repair facilities.

The T-26 tanks' thin armour also proved to be their Achilles' heel, as they showed themselves to be highly vulnerable to towed anti-tank guns provided to the Nationalist side, such as the German 37mm model. Related problems included limited visibility from inside the tank and poor turret ventilation, which reduced crew effectiveness with the prolonged firing of a vehicle's weapons. The flammability of the tank's gasoline-fuelled engine also proved to be a severe problem.

The Red Army experimented with an amphibious version of the T-26, resulting in a small number of prototypes designated as T-26PKh with the suffix letters standing for 'Mobile Underwater'. However, the concept never transitioned to the production stage.

T-26 Improvements

A later-production version of the single-turreted T-26 featured a 45mm main gun and a coaxial 7.62mm machine gun. Its welded armour turret was slightly sloped to provide improved ballistic protection. There also appeared an escape hatch on the hull floor.

Other improvements to the late-production single-turreted T-26s included a more powerful gasoline-powered engine and a more durable suspension system. The exposed overhead vertical engine radiator vent cover on the early-production T-26s (both twin- and single-turreted versions) proved vulnerable to various battlefield threats, including artillery fragments. The solution was a new armoured overhead radiator cover that appeared on single-turreted T-26s beginning in 1939, which drew air through horizontal vents.

Some late-production single-turreted T-26 tanks appeared with 20mm-thick applique armour plates, with an exterior cast-armour gun-shield replacing the original integral welded gun-shield in 1939. Late production single-turreted T-26s left the assembly lines without the rear turret-bustle-mounted 7.62mm machine gun.

T-26 Flame-Thrower Tanks

Soviet industry built a flame-thrower-equipped model of the twin-turreted T-26 labelled the KhT-26, with 552 examples completed between 1932 and 1935. In the process of constructing them one of the two turrets came off on the production line to make room in its hull for the flame-thrower's fuel tanks. The maximum range of the tank's flame-thrower was 44 yards.

Combat usage showed that the KhT-26 was extremely vulnerable after it had exhausted the flame-thrower's fuel supply, as its only other protection was its 7.62mm coaxial machine gun.

A flame-thrower version of the single-turreted T-26 became the KhT-130, with 401 built between 1936 and 1939. Like the KhT-30, the KhT-130 had a coaxial 7.62mm machine gun for self-defence as its 45mm main gun had come off. A new flame-thrower added to the KhT-130 increased the maximum firing range to 58 yards.

With the late-production single-turreted T-26, the Red Army explored the possibility of a flame-thrower version classified as the KhT-131, which retained the 45mm main gun. That configuration proved unworkable due to the existing turret's limited interior space. Therefore the Red Army skipped the 45mm main gun and reverted to the coaxial 7.62mm machine gun arrangement of previous T-26 series flame-thrower tanks. The flame-thrower that went into the T-26 Model 1938 changed the tank's designation to the KhT-132.

In Service Use

According to a Red Army after-action report, T-26 series flame-thrower tanks proved very effective against the Japanese Army during fighting between the two countries in 1938 and 1939. The report also mentioned that the flame-throwers' short range was a tactical shortcoming as it placed the vehicles within range of enemy infantry man-portable weapons.

The T-26 series flame-throwers' short range also proved to be a problem during the First Russo-Finnish War. The tanks had to expose themselves to heavy defensive fire when approaching Finnish Army bunkers. Eventually, the Red Army implemented small-scale combined arms tactics that minimized their flame-thrower tanks' exposure while attempting to approach enemy defensive positions. Despite these changes, the T-26 series flame-thrower tanks suffered much higher losses than their standard single-turreted 45mm main gun-armed counterparts.

As the Red Army wished to retain the 45mm main gun on its single-turreted T-26 series flame-thrower tanks, Soviet industry solved the problem by fitting them with a front hull-mounted flame-thrower. This version was designated the KhT-134. The total number built was 271.

Improvements

By replacing the former horseshoe-shaped metal frame antenna of previous single-turreted T-26 series command tanks with a new steel turret-mounted whip antenna and further strengthening the vehicle's suspension system, the T-26-1 or Model 1 appeared in 1939.

Combat experience gained during the fighting of the First Russo-Finnish War resulted in some Red Army light tanks, such as the single-turreted T-26s, appearing with bolt-on applique armour plates on both turrets and hull.

T-26 Summary

The Red Army took into service about 11,000 examples of the T-26 series before ending production in January 1941. During the 1930s the T-26 series was considered a capable tank; however, it was obsolete when the Germans invaded the Soviet Union. Despite this, the T-26 series was the most numerous tanks in the Red Army's inventory. Unfortunately, one-third of those tanks were inoperative when the Germans invaded.

In theory, the T-26 series' 45mm main gun was equal to the 50mm main gun on some German Panzer III medium tanks. Unfortunately Soviet industry could not produce enough armour-piercing (AP) rounds. Making matters worse, those supplied to the Red Army suffered from severe quality control problems, resulting in defective anti-tank rounds. Combined with the German tank's superior optics and radios, these factors gave the German Panzer III medium tank a significant edge over T-26 series tanks on the battlefields of 1941.

T-50 Light Tank

Before the German invasion, the Red Army sought a suitable replacement for the T-26 series. What eventually appeared was the Soviet-designed and built four-man, diesel-engine-powered T-50 light tank armed with a 45mm main gun.

Riding on a torsion bar suspension system, the T-50 had a three-man turret crew, in contrast to all the earlier Red Army light tanks with a one- or two-man turret crew. Maximum armour protection on the 15-ton vehicle was 37mm on the turret's front.

Unfortunately, the T-50 proved more complicated and costly to build than initially anticipated, with only sixty-three examples completed before the Red Army ordered production stopped in February 1942.

Under the Table Tank

Besides acquiring British tank designs during the 1930s for study and possible licence production, the Red Army was not averse to using subterfuge with regard to existing foreign tank designs of interest. One of these proved to be a series of prototype tank designs that had sprung forth from the fertile imagination of American inventor J. Walter Christie.

Christie's prototype gasoline-engine-powered tanks had a suspension system based on helically-wound coil springs acting independently on large road wheels. This innovative new suspension system allowed his prototype tanks to reach unheard-of speeds for their day.

Another innovative design feature of Christie's prototype tanks that caught the Red Army's attention was his development of a convertible track system. In this context, the term convertible meant that a tank could run on its tracks when travelling off-road, but on its large, rubber-rimmed road wheels when running on paved roads instead of on its tracks.

A tank's ability to operate without its tracks in the 1930s was a central selling-point. It could help overcome the lack of durability of the existing steel track designs that resulted in a short lifespan, making convertible tanks an attractive option.

The Red Army's Christie Tank

With the co-operation of Christie, the Red Army bought two examples of one of his numerous designs. In this case, it was a vehicle he labelled the M1940 Convertible Tank. They were shipped to the Soviet Union in December 1930 without their one-man turrets and labelled as agricultural tractors. Christie's arrangement with the Red Army had not gone unnoticed and there were some efforts by the United States War Department and the American State Department to block the sale, all to no avail.

Upon the Model 1940s' arrival in the Soviet Union, Soviet industry quickly copied them and designed and built new turrets for the vehicles. The Red Army's first production version of Christie's convertible tank came off the factory floor in November 1931. It received the designation BT-2 Model 1932. The prefix letters 'BT' are the Russian abbreviation for fast tank or high-speed tank.

The Red Army's BT-2 tanks originally received power from rebuilt gasoline-powered aircraft engines obtained through Soviet intermediaries operating a sham import and export company in the US. Eventually, Soviet industry began building their version of the American aircraft engine for the BT-2.

The Red Army had initially called for 900 examples of the BT-2 to be built. That number was later reduced to a more manageable 482 examples following a more realistic appraisal of Soviet industry's capabilities. Armour protection for the BT-2 topped out at 13mm on the turret front.

The BT-2 in service proved unimpressive, with a long list of design issues that needed correction, mainly resulting from Soviet industry copying an immature prototype tank design and rushing it into production.

BT-2 Armament Confusion

The original Red Army intention revolved around mounting a French-derived 37mm gun in the BT-2's two-man turret. That later changed to a more powerful licence-built copy of a German-designed 37mm gun. As the turrets for the BT-2 were designed for the smaller French gun, the larger German gun left no room for a coaxial 7.62mm machine gun. A ball mount for a 7.62mm machine gun eventually appeared on the turret's right side in place of a coaxial position.

Another effort involved trying to fit the turret of the BT-2 tank with a 45mm main gun. That effort went nowhere as the BT-2 turret proved too small for the larger gun. Therefore the Red Army had Soviet industry go back to arming the tank with the smaller German 37mm gun. However, the production of the gun had not kept up with the number of BT-2s built.

Of approximately 600 examples of the BT-2 constructed by 1933, there were 37mm guns for only about half of them. Therefore the Red Army decided to arm the remaining BT-2 tanks with a gun mount with two 7.62mm machine guns. These machine gun-armed BT-2 tanks would see combat during the First Russo-Finish War and the period immediately following the German invasion of the Soviet Union.

Additional BT Versions

With lessons learned from the BT-2, the next version that came off the assembly lines bore the designation BT-5. The 13-ton vehicle featured a larger turret armed with a 45mm main gun and dispensed with the ball-mounted 7.62mm machine gun fitted in the turret's right front. In its place there appeared a 7.62mm coaxial machine gun. A total of 1,946 examples of the BT-5 came off the assembly lines, with 325 equipped with radios.

The replacement for the BT-5 Model 1932 would be the approximately 16-ton BT-7, which retained the layout of the earlier tank but differed as it had a redesigned turret and hull of all-welded construction rather than the riveted construction seen on the earlier BTs. Instead of using the Soviet copy of the American-designed gasoline-powered engine from the BT-2 and BT-5, the BT-7 received power from a German-designed gasoline-powered engine copied by Soviet industry, which completed 2,596 examples of the BT-7.

With a new welded turret featuring sloped armour, similar to that on the late-production single-turreted T-26s, the BT-7 went into production. The concept of sloping tank armour to improve its ballistic strength came from the French industry's pioneering interwar work. Some late-production BT-7s appeared with a 7.62mm machine gun in a ball mount in the turret rear.

Some of the radio-equipped versions of the BT-7 appeared with new steel whip antennas rather than the previous horseshoe-shaped metal frame antennas. There were 2,017 radio-equipped examples of the BT-7 designated the BT-7RT.

BT-7M

The final version of the BT series designated as the BT-7M was almost identical to the late-production BT-7s, with some minor differences. These included re-designed turret hatches that allowed for a ring mount, labelled the P-40, that mounted a 7.62mm machine gun intended for anti-aircraft protection. In this configuration, the vehicle was sometimes unofficially designated the BT-8.

The most significant change to the BT-7M was a diesel-powered engine that significantly increased the vehicle's maximum operational range due to diesel fuel's greater thermal efficiency than gasoline.

Increased protection for the BT-7M crew also came from up-armouring that pushed the turret front's maximum armour thickness to 22mm. Due to the weight gain from up-armouring, the BT-7M lost the ability to run on its road wheels. However, the Red Army no longer considered that ability to be necessary for a tank's design. Production of the BT-7M concluded in 1941, with 788 examples coming out of the factory doors.

BT Series Summary

Fifty examples of the BT-5 were supplied to the Republican forces during the Spanish Civil War by the Soviet government. Like the T-26 series tanks provided earlier to the Republicans, the BT-5 was far superior to the machine gun-armed tanks/tankettes supplied to the Nationalist forces. Unfortunately, like the T-26, the BT-5's thin armour was compounded by the Republican military leadership's lack of experience using armoured units and the BT-5s found themselves need-lessly squandered in poorly-planned and poorly-conducted battles.

The Red Army's BT-5s and BT-7s would also see combat against the Japanese Army in the Far East in 1938 and 1939. During these clashes, the T-26 series and the BT series gasoline-engine-powered version's vulnerability to enemy anti-tank weapons and their propensity to burn caught the Red Army senior leadership's attention. No doubt this influenced the Red Army's eventual adoption of better-armoured diesel-engine-powered tanks.

The T-26 series as well as BT-5s and BT-7s would also participate in the Red Army's invasion of eastern Poland (17 September 1939 to 6 October 1941) and during the First Russo-Finnish War. The former cost the Red Army more tanks than anticipated, while the latter proved to be a dismal failure on every level.

The German invasion of the Soviet Union quickly overwhelmed the Red Army. In the process of trying to stem the enemy's advance it lost the majority of its prewar tank fleet, including the bulk of its BT series tanks. Most fell victim to mechanical issues, including running out of fuel and then combat action. Some BT series tanks survived in the Far East to participate in the Red Army invasion of Japanese-occupied Manchuria (9 to 20 August 1945).

A contributing reason for the continuing failure of the Red Army leadership to properly employ its armoured forces during its initial invasion of Finland or during the German invasion was a lack of understanding of its requirements in battle. Author Roger R. Reese in his book *The Soviet Military Experience: A History of the Soviet Army 1917–1991* summarized comments made on 5 August 1941 in a report by a senior Red Army general:

> Ignorant of the maintenance and resupply requirements of armored vehicles [Red] army staffs made no provisions in their battle plans for mechanized units to perform routine but vital maintenance and resupply their fuel and ammunition – a far more complex and time-consuming undertaking for armored units than for the more familiar infantry. The special staff officers of army headquarters assigned to oversee the needs of mechanized forces failed to bring these needs to the attention of their commanders, who kept desperately throwing their armored forces into the breach with less effectiveness and greater losses each time.

Deep Battle

In the 1920s and early 1930s, some senior Red Army generals began to put forth a new and very controversial combined arms offensive doctrine called 'Deep Battle'. From the 1936 Red Army Field Regulations appears the following translated extract on the concept:

> Modern combat matériel makes possible the simultaneous destruction of the enemy at all echelons. There is an increase in the options for re-organization, surprising flank movements, and occupation of areas behind enemy lines with attacks against his escape routes. When the enemy is attacked, he must be surrounded and completely destroyed.

A vital element of the Red Army's plans to implement Deep Battle involved tanks, divided originally into three types: immediate infantry support tanks (NNP), long-range infantry support tanks (DPP) and long-range action tanks

---

(DD). The letter designations are abbreviations of the Russian language names for the tank types.

The original role envisioned for the NNP tanks involved breaching the enemy's most forward defensive line (with the aid of artillery) to allow passage of the first echelon of Red Army infantry formations. If the enemy's defences proved too challenging for the tanks, the infantry would take the lead under the tanks' protective fire until a breakthrough occurred. A secondary role for the NNP tanks was fending off enemy counterattacks.

The vehicles categorized as DPP tanks had the same job as the NNP tanks. The difference is that they led the second echelon of advancing Red Army infantry formations during a breakthrough of enemy lines. Once through the enemy's front lines, they were tasked with attacking enemy artillery positions and preventing the enemy from reinforcing his front-line positions.

The DD tanks had the job of passing through any penetration of the enemy's front line achieved by the NNP and DPP tanks. Once these tanks were 6 to 9 miles behind enemy lines, Deep Battle transitioned to 'Deep Operation'. The DD tanks were to drive deep into the enemy's rear areas, raising havoc among the enemy's command and control sites and supply points.

DD tanks made up the exploitation echelon (mobile groups). They were to have a wide degree of independence from the other arms of the Red Army to allow them to pursue opportunities that arose which might increase their battlefield success and hasten the enemy's defeat. One Red Army general stated in 1933 that he believed the DD tanks could reach as far as 19 to 25 miles behind enemy lines within the first twenty-four hours.

Due to unresolved issues with Deep Battle and Deep Operation, the Red Army never developed satisfactory solutions for supplying its DD tank spearheads with the fuel and ammunition they would require when behind enemy lines if the fighting continued for more than three days.

Another problem was the limited numbers of radios produced by Soviet industry, which in turn meant that command and control of far-flung DD tank formations might be problematic.

The implementation of the Deep Battle and Deep Operation doctrine prewar proved difficult for the Red Army. Soviet industry could not build as many tanks as needed. The Red Army also lacked the trained manpower from the lowest ranks up to the most senior level to successfully put into practice the complex combined arms arrangements called for in Deep Battle as demonstrated in prewar training exercises.

A Red Army report dated April 1933 contains an extract written by an inspector from the Directorate of Motorization and Mechanization (UMM). It reports what he learned from talking to the staff of various armoured units during a training exercise:

> ... [they] do not have even the most elementary knowledge of the action of the vehicle [tank] as part of a platoon or about tank groups NPP, DPP and

DD. For instance, in the 7th Company, they did not even know about the existence of published tank manuals, instructions and so on.

In subsequent Red Army training exercises, the results appeared promising. One Red Army general suggested that an attack begins with DPP tanks dealing with enemy towed anti-tank guns and machine guns. By so doing, the follow-on DD tanks would suffer fewer losses as they raced into the enemy's rear areas.

Another Red Army general recommended that with sufficient artillery support, the DD tanks could head toward the enemy's rear areas without severe losses. Someone else put forward the idea that only NPP and DD tank units were required, skipping the DPP echelon. Eventually, the NNP and DPP tank formation distinctions disappeared, with just the labels DD and PD remaining.

Those in the Red Army senior levels who did not endorse the concept of Deep Battle or DD tanks wished to keep them subordinated to the Red Army's cavalry and infantry branches. They also remained convinced that modern towed anti-tank guns and artillery would blunt any far-ranging offensive advance by DD tanks. The only exceptions would occur when there was favourable terrain or a lack of creditable enemy defences.

The symbolic nail in the coffin for the Deep Battle doctrine in the Red Army occurred in 1937 when Joseph Stalin began purging the army's leadership. The purges quickly decimated the ranks of all those who had worked so hard to bring the Deep Battle doctrine to fruition.

In a turn of events, Stalin and the post-purge Red Army leadership would embrace the doctrine of Deep Battle and Deep Operation in 1944. The Red Army finally possessed both the equipment and experienced senior leadership to put the once discredited doctrine into successful practice.

(**Above**) During the Russian Civil War (1917–24), the Red Army captured a small number of French FT-17 light tanks in various states of disrepair. These had been supplied to the anti-Bolshevik forces (referred to as the 'Whites') by the French government. To build up its tank strength the Red Army tasked Soviet industry to reverse-engineer the FT-17, producing the example pictured here. Approximately a dozen eventually came off the factory floor, with the first delivered in August 1920. (*Dreamstime*)

(**Opposite, above**) Following construction of the reverse-engineered French FT-17 light tanks, Soviet industry built a new light tank based on what they learned from the FT-17. The result was the MS-1 pictured here, also known as the T18. It was armed with a 37mm main gun. In general, the MS-1 was very similar to the FT-17 but had a new suspension system. Production of the MS-1 began in 1928 and continued until 1931, with approximately 959 examples constructed. (*Dreamstime*)

(**Opposite, below**) The Red Army began buying foreign-designed tanks and armoured fighting vehicles for inspiration during the interwar period. Among those brought to the Soviet Union for technical evaluation was the British two-man machine gun-armed Carden Loyd Mark VI Tankette. Based on that vehicle, Soviet industry began building a copy as seen here, labelled the T-27. Between 1931 and 1933 a total of 3,328 examples came off the Soviet assembly lines. (*Dreamstime*)

(**Above**) Besides the British two-man machine gun-armed Carden Loyd Mark VI Tank-ette, the Red Army also purchased the Vickers-Armstrong Carden Loyd Amphibious Tank, Model 1931. Soviet industry used the British vehicle as a starting-point to develop the T-37A amphibious light tank, with a captured example seen here in Finnish Army service. Production of the gasoline-engine-powered machine gun-armed tank took place between 1933 and 1936, with approximately 2,000 examples built. (*SA-Kuva*)

(**Above**) A pristine T-38 amphibious light tank is seen here taking part in a parade of historical Red Army tanks. It was a modernized version of the T-37A with a wider and lower hull. The T-38's one-man turret and driver's position were on the opposite side of the hull from their positions on its predecessor. The reason for the switch is lost to history. The T-38 came off the assembly lines between 1936 and 1937 with 1,288 being built. It initially saw combat during the First Russo-Finnish War and the early months of the German invasion. (*Dreamstime*)

(**Opposite, below**) Before the German invasion, Soviet industry managed to complete 221 examples of the new amphibious light tank pictured here and labelled the T-40. It was to replace the T-37A and the T-38 and came with two machine guns. Like previous Red Army amphibious light tanks, the majority of T-40s lacked radios, making their battle-field effectiveness in the reconnaissance role questionable. (*Author's collection*)

(**Above**) Following the German invasion, the Red Army cancelled further production of the T-40 amphibious light tank. However, such was the need for any tanks that the Red Army had industry build 335 examples of a non-amphibious version of the T-40 as seen here, armed with a 20mm main gun and a coaxial 7.62mm machine gun. The T-40 and its non-amphibious replacement rode on a torsion bar suspension system instead of the coil springs used on the T-37A and T-38. (*Dreamstime*)

(**Opposite, above**) Prior to the German invasion, Soviet industry was developing a non-amphibious light tank seen here and designated the T-60. Lacking an amphibious capability, the tank was cheaper and faster to build. The two-man T-60 had a 20mm main gun as its main armament, supplemented by a coaxial 7.62mm machine gun. Production began in July 1941 and continued until September 1942, with around 6,000 examples coming off the factory floor. (*Dreamstime*)

(**Opposite, below**) The Red Army's planned replacement for the two-man T-60 light tank was the up-armoured two-man T-70 light tank, which quickly evolved into the improved two-man T-70M pictured here. Armed with a 47mm main gun and a coaxial 7.62mm machine gun, it had a maximum armour thickness of 50mm on the turret front. By comparison, the T-60 had a maximum frontal armour thickness of 35mm. (*Dreamstime*)

(**Above**) Power for the T-70M pictured here came from two gasoline engines, providing it with a top speed on level roads of 28mph. The tank's maximum range could be as far as 200 miles. Production began in March 1942 and continued until October 1943, with approximately 8,000 constructed. It had a length of around 14ft, a width of about 7ft and a height of roughly 7ft. (*Dreamstime*)

(**Opposite, above**) Combat experience soon made it clear to the Red Army that the single-man turrets on all its light tanks were unsatisfactory. Stationed in the turrets, platoon commanders and company commanders could not operate their tank's weapons and also direct other tanks' actions. This led the Red Army to have Soviet industry build a modified T-70M with a larger two-man turret. That vehicle became the T-80 light tank appearing in this photograph. However, only seventy-five examples of the T-80 appeared before the Red Army gave up on fielding additional new light tanks in October 1943. (*Dreamstime*)

(**Opposite, below**) Among the British-designed and built tanks the Red Army acquired before the Second World War were fifteen examples of the three-man Vickers 6-Ton Tank (also known as the Vickers Mark E Tank). It came in both a single-turreted version as seen here and a twin-turreted configuration. Preferring the twin-turreted version, the Red Army ordered a licence-built version incorporating Soviet modifications, which became the T-26 light tank. (*Dreamstime*)

(**Above**) Pictured here during prewar training is an early-production T-26 light tank with its two machine gun-armed turrets. Vickers could sell its Six-Ton Tank to the Soviet Union because the British Army had rejected the vehicle due to concerns about durability of the tank's suspension system. Around 1,600 twin-turreted T-26s came off the factory floor between 1931 and 1934. (*Author's collection*)

(**Opposite, above**) The Red Army decided to have one in five of its twin-turreted T-26 light tanks fitted with a 37mm gun. A museum example of that configuration is pictured here. Around 400 of 1,600 twin-turreted T-26 light tanks built featured the 37mm gun mounted in the right-hand turret. Most of these tanks' 37mm guns were a modified version of a French design, with a much smaller number armed with a licence-built copy of a German-designed 37mm gun. (*Dreamstime*)

(**Opposite, below**) The Red Army quickly realized that the single-man turrets of the early-production T-26s lacked adequate interior space to properly service a 37mm gun properly. In 1932 it tasked Soviet industry with designing a larger two-man turret that could accommodate a 45mm gun, an example of which is pictured here. The gun itself was an up-scaled version of a licence-built German-designed towed 37mm anti-tank gun. (*Dreamstime*)

(**Opposite, above**) This picture taken during the First Russo-Finnish War (1939–40) shows a knocked-out mid-production single-turreted T-26 light tank armed with a 45mm main gun. This configuration proved the most numerous T-26 series tank built, with 5,500 examples coming off the assembly lines between 1933 and 1936. (*SA-Kuva*)

(**Opposite, below**) The T-26 light tanks in the foreground are radio-equipped command tanks, as evidenced by the metal frame antennas surrounding their turrets. Unfortunately, such a prominent external feature would quickly identify the tank's purpose and result in the enemy targeting it for early destruction. Steel whip antennas did not appear until early 1939 on Red Army tanks. (*Author's collection*)

(**Above**) The vehicle commander and driver of a radio-equipped T-26 light tank talk to a civilian in this posed image. The mid-production T-26s armed with a 45mm gun proved to be the most numerous in the Red Army's arsenal when the Germans invaded, with most lost in the first few months of the fighting. The T-26 had a length of about 15ft, a width of around 8ft and a height of roughly 7ft. Its 95hp gasoline engine provided a top speed on level roads of about 20mph. (*Author's collection*)

(**Opposite, above**) The prewar Red Army was a firm believer in the effectiveness of flame-thrower-armed tanks. However, combat experience gained during the First Russo-Finnish War demonstrated that the range of the T-26's flame gun was too short, and the vehicles' thin armour therefore made them too vulnerable. To rectify that issue, the Red Army began up-armouring its flame-thrower tanks. It also fielded radio-controlled flame-thrower tanks. (*Dreamstime*)

(**Opposite, below**) A problem for early- and mid-production T-26 series tanks (as already mentioned) was their thin armour protection. One solution involved sloping the armour on the turrets of late-production T-26s as seen here. In addition, sloped 20mm-thick spaced armour plates were added to the vertical upper hull sides of late-production T-26s. Sloping armour provides an improved degree of ballistic protection without using thicker and, by default, heavier armour. (*Dreamstime*)

(**Above**) The curved box-like structure protruding from this late-production T-26 light tank's rear engine deck is a cowling covering the engine air intake. The tank's trans-mission is in the lower front hull of the vehicle, therefore the drive sprockets are at the front of the suspension system and the idler at the rear. The armour on the front of the turret and hull is 20mm thick, with the turret and upper hull sides 15mm thick. As can be observed, the suspension system on the T-26 series consisted of two groups of four bogie wheels on either side of the hull. The bogie wheels themselves were sprung on quarter elliptic leaf springs. The maximum range of the T-26 series was approximately 200 miles. (*Dreamstime*)

(**Above**) A late-production Red Army T-26 light tank is seen here in Finnish Army service. The vehicle commander doubled as the loader. Note that the vehicle commander's overhead hatch opens forward. The tank had authorized storage for 205 main gun rounds and about 3,000 7.62mm rounds for the vehicle's machine guns. Some late-production Red Army T-26s had, in addition to the coaxial machine gun, a second machine gun in the rear of the turret bustle. Some featured an additional roof-mounted 7.62mm machine gun. (*SA-Kuva*)

(**Opposite, above**) The Red Army's planned replacement for the T-26 was the better-armoured T-50 light tank pictured here. Like the T-26, the vehicle has a 45mm main gun. Its diesel engine and torsion bar suspension system provided a top speed on level surfaces of 37mph. Another significant change from earlier light tanks was its three-man turret with a vision cupola for the vehicle commander. Despite its modern features, the Red Army cancelled production after only sixty-nine examples were built due to the decision to concentrate on medium and heavy tanks. (*Dreamstime*)

(**Opposite, below**) The Red Army became enthralled in the 1930s with a tracked chassis designed by American inventor J. Walter Christie. The vehicle's ability to operate with or without its tracks at high speeds seemed an attractive option as tank tracks of the day were not very durable. The Red Army purchased two of Christie's vehicles and quickly copied them. With the addition of a two-man 37mm gun-armed turret, the vehicle became the BT-2 pictured here. BT is the Russian language acronym for *Bystrokhodny* tank, which translates as 'Fast Tank'. (*Author's collection*)

The Red Army considered the BT-2's 37mm main gun to be inadequate. It therefore had Soviet industry design a new turret armed with a 45mm main gun as seen here. With this new turret, the vehicle became the BT-5 with the first series production examples appearing in 1933. The metal frame antenna identifies this tank as a command vehicle. (*Author's collection*)

The BT-5 appeared with two different types of turrets, with the trackless example pictured here having a welded turret sporting a pronounced rear bustle. A smaller number of BT-5 turrets were riveted and had a more compact rectangular rear bustle. A few of these riveted turrets went onto T-26 light tanks. The BT-5, like the BT-2, had a gasoline-powered engine that provided a maximum speed on level roads of approximately 45mph and an operational range of about 100 miles. (*Dreamstime*)

A distinguishing design feature of the BT-2 and BT-5 was the driver's sizeable two-piece hatch seen here with a driver posing for the photographer. It projected out from the vehicle's sloped glacis and included the upper hull's front portion, which contained the driver's direct-view vision block. While providing the tank's driver with relatively easy ingress and egress, it was a ballistic weak spot and allowed bullet splash to enter the vehicle. (*Author's collection*)

(**Above**) A Red Army BT-5 knocked out during the First Russo-Finnish War (1939–40). Note how the lower front hull narrows. That design feature allowed the two unpowered front road wheels to be turned left and right when the tank was running trackless. Power for the vehicle when running trackless came from the two rear hull drive sprockets. In the trackless configuration drivers used a steering wheel. When the tracks went back on the tank the driver removed the steering wheel and reverted to the standard clutch and brake steering system. (*SA-Kuva*)

(**Opposite, above**) The BT-2 and BT-5 received power from either reconditioned 400hp American-designed and built V-12 Liberty gasoline engines or a Soviet industry copy. Due to shortages of both engines, Soviet industry switched to building a copy of a more powerful 500hp German-designed aircraft engine. That engine went into the modified hull of a BT-5 that had a rounded lower front hull and received the designation BT-7. The early-production example pictured here came off the factory floor with a BT-5 turret. (*Dreamstime*)

(**Opposite, below**) Pictured here is a late-production BT-7 with the new sloped-armour turret armed with a 45mm main gun. It started coming off the assembly lines in September 1939; its frontal armour was increased from 17mm to 22mm thick. In the foreground, three junior Red Army officers study a map. Enlisted men in the Red Army were neither allowed to have maps nor taught how to use them. (*Author's collection*)

An example of a late-production BT-7 with its sloped armoured turret is pictured here. It lacks the rear turret bustle-mounted 7.62mm machine gun seen on some BT-7s. Power for the tank came from a Soviet industry copy of a German 500hp gasoline-powered aviation engine. Plans called for the engine's eventual replacement by a diesel engine but that proved a design dead end, with only nine built between 1938 and 1939. (*Dreamstime*)

Two German soldiers pose in front of a knocked-out BT-7 with the late-production sloped turret design. Due to the prewar light tanks' proclivity for mechanical break-downs, the Red Army leadership minimized their use. The downside is that their crews had little chance to train on them and their officers never learned how to employ them in battle. Adding to the problem was the fact that the Red Army leadership was more interested in overall tank numbers and paid less heed to having a sufficient stockpile of spare parts on hand. (*Author's collection*)

Chapter Three

Medium Tanks

The initial medium tanks in the Red Army proved to be captured examples of the First World War-vintage British-designed and built Mark A named 'the Whippet'. These were supplied to anti-Bolshevik forces during the Russian Civil War (1917–22) by the British government. They would last in Red Army service until a shortage of spare parts rendered them inoperative by the early 1920s.

T-28 Medium Tank

The first indigenous Soviet-designed medium tank considered a success was the gasoline-engine-powered T-28. The six-man 34-ton tank featured three turrets: two 7.62mm machine gun-armed one-man turrets with limited traverse at the tank's front and a larger, two-man 76.2mm gun-armed turret with 360 degrees of traverse located behind and above the two machine gun-armed turrets.

Instead of having a coaxially-mounted 7.62mm coaxial machine gun, the T-28 main turret featured a separate ball-mounted 7.62mm machine gun on the right front of the vehicle's turret. Maximum armour thickness on the front of the main turret was 30mm.

A later-production example of the T-28 sported a longer-barrelled 76.2mm main gun. Some T-28 series tanks had a 7.62mm machine gun mounted in the main turret's rear bustle and another on the roof for anti-aircraft protection.

T-28 Service Use

Between 1934 and 1940 there were 503 examples of the T-28 series built. They would first see combat during the Red Army invasion of Eastern Poland in September 1939. Combat experience gained during the First Russo-Finnish War quickly highlighted that the T-28 was badly under-armoured. To rectify this issue, the Red Army had Soviet industry mount applique armour to the tank's turrets, raising the vehicle's weight to 35 tons.

Those T-28 series tanks that survived the First Russo-Finnish War would face the German Army in 1941. Most, however, were lost to non-combat causes such as mechanical failure or fuel shortages. A few would remain in service long enough to be involved in Moscow's defence (September 1941 to April 1942) and Leningrad's siege (September 1941 to January 1944) during its early stage.

The A-20 Appears

The Red Army leadership had the foresight in 1937 to realize that its existing inventory of medium tanks was obsolete. Therefore it tasked the Kharkov Locomotive Factory (KhPZ) design bureau, under the supervision of engineers

Mikhail Koshkin and his second-in-command Alexander A. Morozov, to develop a new medium tank. What appeared in response became the prototype A-20 armed with a 45mm main gun. The prefix letter 'A' meant that the vehicle was a prototype.

A proposed version of the A-20 with a track-only suspension system became the A-20G; the suffix letter 'G' meant tracked. Without a convertible wheel/track system requirement, the designers intended to make the hulls wider, allowing for more onboard ammunition stowage. The weight saved by not having the Christie-type convertible wheel/track system was used to up-armour the tank.

There also appeared a proposal that the A-20G should feature a 76.2mm main gun. The Red Army organization responsible for tank development proved interested and recommended its further development on 6 September 1938, along with thicker armour.

Another change with the A-20G was a V-12 diesel engine labelled the 'V-2', initially developed for the BT-7M light tank. A novel design feature of the diesel engine was its lightweight aluminium engine block.

Pushing the A-20G Along

During a two-day meeting in Moscow in early December 1938, Koshkin and Morozov presented Stalin and an assortment of high-ranking military and civilians the plans and wooden models of the proposed A-20 and A-20G. Most present preferred the more conventional A-20. However, Stalin saw merit in the A-20G and authorized the construction of prototypes of both vehicles.

The prototypes went off to a Red Army proving ground in July 1939 to determine the superior vehicle. The all-tracked A-20G proved almost as fast on level roads as the A-20 was running on road wheels, i.e. without its tracks. It also proved superior off-road to the A-20 when both vehicles were riding on tracks.

The all-track A-20G eventually received the designation of the A-32 #1. Its superior off-road mobility came from having five road wheels per side rather than the four road wheels per side of the A-20, therefore providing a better distribution of weight and, in turn, decreasing its ground pressure.

The official in charge of the initial Red Army trials of the A-20 and the A-32 #1 issued a final report in late August 1939 stating that both vehicles were equally effective. One can only suppose that he feared offending anybody with his choice and decided to play it safe, leading to the second round of trials.

Soviet Design Bureaus

Soviet design bureaus and their affiliated production plants were state-owned and supposedly state-directed. However, they often tended to act more like capitalistic companies heavily influenced by their founder's visions, leadership and political talents. The arrangement allowed for a degree of initiative in designing weapons such as tanks, overcoming the typical reactionary opinions expressed by the more conservative senior Soviet military establishment.

During the second round of trials beginning in September 1939, Koshkin arranged to demonstrate the A-20 and A-32 #1 to high-ranking military and civilians on 22 September 1939. The demonstration was a success and a draft decree came a few days later, accepting both the A-20 and A-32 #1 for Red Army service.

The decree called for ten pilot A-20s to be completed by 1 January 1940, and full-scale production to start by 1 March 1940. Pilots are proof-of-concept vehicles intended to demonstrate that a production line is capable of building an object.

The Red Army also wanted ten pilots of an up-armoured and up-gunned A-32 #1 with a 76.2mm main gun by 1 June 1940, with full-scale production to begin on the same day.

Taking Matters into His Own Hands

Koshkin, on his own initiative, decided to emphasize an increased level of protection with a second A-32 prototype referred to as the A-32 #2. With only a slight loss of mobility, the additional armour on the latter brought the vehicle's weight up to 22 tons.

As the A-20 and A-32 #1 prototypes underwent testing which ended in August 1939, Koshkin ordered enough extra weight added to the A-32 #2 to simulate having frontal armour 45mm thick and a 76.2mm main gun. Trials in late August 1939 demonstrated that the extra 4 tons of weight had little effect on the A-32 #2's mobility, prompting Koshkin to try interesting the Red Army in the tank, which then became the A-34.

A Change in Plans

The reality of modern warfare intruded on the Red Army's plans for producing the A-20 and A-32 #1 when the Russo-Finish War broke out at the end of November 1939. It quickly became apparent that the existing light and medium tanks were badly under-armoured compared to the capabilities of the latest anti-tank guns. They also lacked the firepower required to destroy well-built Finnish Army bunkers. In response to the poor showing of its tanks in Finland, the Red Army cancelled the A-20 programme on 9 December 1939 and instead an order for 220 examples of the A-32 #1 appeared.

Koshkin had still not received approval from the Soviet defence minister to place the better-armed and armoured A-34 into production. The defence minister kept raising bureaucratic roadblocks delaying considering the A-34 as he favoured the KV-1 heavy tank proposed by his son-in-law's factory.

To counter the obstacles put in place by the defence minister, Koshkin arranged for a publicity stunt involving the two prototype A-34s. They were driven from the factory in Leningrad to Moscow for inspection by Stalin and other high-ranking officials in early March 1940.

In conjunction with further demonstrations, the stunt worked. The Soviet defence minister conceded the A-34's capabilities and subsequently authorized its production on 31 March 1940. By this time the vehicle had already become known as the 'T-34'.

The Red Army placed an initial order for 600 T-34s, with construction to begin in June 1940 and another 2,800 examples set for completion in 1941. As events unfolded, only 115 of the T-34 tanks ordered for 1940 came out of the factories beginning in September 1940. The tanks weighed about 29 tons.

Koshkin, who took part in the prototypes' demonstrations, caught pneumonia during the endeavours and died in September 1940. His deputy, Alexander Morozov, replaced him as head of the design team.

Last-Minute Concerns

An impressive showing put on by the two T-34 prototypes during trials appears in a Red Army report: 'In armor protection, firepower and performance in wintry conditions, the T-34 is significantly superior to the existing [Red Army] tanks in service.' The same report also mentioned shortcomings with the T-34 prototypes' design that needed addressing.

One issue revolved around the T-34 prototype's small cramped turret. The larger 76.2mm main gun made it extremely difficult for the two-person turret crew to effectively service the weapon and use the turret's observation and sighting devices; a partial solution was found by widening the turret by around 6in.

Inside the Turret

Because the T-34 series tanks lacked a turret basket, the loader had to move around inside the tank to follow the breech of the main gun as the turret traversed. The loader was also responsible for the coaxial 7.62mm machine gun. His position on the right side of the main gun breech was the opposite of the turret crew arrangement of American and German medium tanks.

When not engaged in loading the main gun, the loader sat on a seat attached to the interior of the turret ring. The vehicle commander had a seat on the left-hand side of the gun breech. Like the loader's seat, the vehicle commander's seat was itself attached to the turret ring.

Vision Devices

The optical devices on the prototype T-34s had issues. These included large dead spaces around the vehicle, rapid fogging on the lenses and cracking with the firing of the tank's main gun. A British military report dated February 1944 on a T-34 supplied by the Soviet Union includes the following extract regarding the tank's periscopes: 'The quality of the glass is poor and contains many bubbles and flaws.'

In the book titled *T-34 in Action: Soviet Tank Troops in WWII*, many a former Red Army tanker mentioned that as the driver's hatch-mounted periscopes were so poor, they kept their hatches partly open in battle so they could see where they were going. A second reason for keeping the front hatch partially open in battle was to bring in fresh air to help clear the tank's interior of the toxic gases generated by the firing of the main gun and onboard machine guns.

Early Soviet tank optical sights reflected far less light than their German counterparts, putting T-34 tank crews at a major disadvantage when engaging enemy tanks. By copying German optical sights, Soviet industry began to catch up in quality by 1943.

Problems Remain

In response to the shortcomings noted with the two T-34 prototypes in trials the factory made changes, but many of the prototypes' problems remained. These issues appear in the conclusions of the following December 1940 report, which involved testing three early-production T-34s from October to December 1940:

1. The lack of space for the crew in the fighting compartment caused by the small size of the turret based on the turret ring.
2. The inconvenience of using the ammunition load, which is stowed on the floor of the fighting compartment (in eight non-armored containers covered by a removable rubberized matting with a smaller number of main rounds stored along the interior walls of the fighting compartment).
3. Delay in shifting fire as a result of the inconvenient position of the turret's traversing mechanism (either manual or electrically powered).
4. The absence of visual contact between the tanks while executing a fire mission because the sole device that permits all-round vision – the PT-6 sight – is used only for aiming.
5. The impossibility of using the TOD-6 sight as a result of the obstruction of its angles of sight's scale with the PT-6 sight.
6. The significant and slowly subsiding rocking of the tank when moving negatively affects the accuracy of fire from the cannon and machine gun.

Firepower

The initial 1940 series production T-34s featured a 76.2mm main gun designated the L-11, designed in 1938. Its performance was considered lacking due to its low muzzle velocity of only 1,825ft/s. The introduction of the longer-barrelled F-34 main gun in 1941 solved the problem. The longer barrel meant higher muzzle velocities and, in turn, better armour penetration abilities and more accuracy.

By August 1943, it became clear to Red Army tankers that the F-34 gun lacked the penetrative ability to deal with up-armoured German medium and heavy tanks that began appearing in ever-increasing numbers in the summer of 1943. Despite that, the F-34 remained in use until the last examples of the 76.2mm gun-armed T-34 series came off the assembly lines in 1944.

The standard steel armour-piercing (AP) round fired from the T-34's F-34 main gun had a muzzle velocity of 2,172ft/s. In trials it demonstrated that it could

---

T-34 Designations

The Red Army generally did not assign designations to the various subvariants of the T-34 tank series. The Germans did, however, apply suffix letters to identify T-34 subvariants in their military reports. Contemporary military authors have taken to describing T-34 subvariants by the year authorizing their production. Wartime Red Army tankers simply called it the 'Thirty-Four'.

penetrate 60mm of armour sloped at 30 degrees at a range of 437 yards. At a range of 875 yards, the same round could penetrate 50mm thick armour sloped at 30 degrees.

A tungsten-cored subcalibre round for the F-34 cannon began appearing in the summer of 1943. The Red Army referred to it as a 'subcalibre projectile'. In the British Army, the ammo was labelled as an armour-piercing discarding sabot (APDS) round. The US Army referred to APDS rounds as Hyper-Velocity Armour-Piercing (HVAP) rounds.

Protection

The T-34 turrets were initially constructed of rolled homogenous armour (RHA) plates welded together. A disadvantage of RHA is its inability to be easily formed into shapes other than flat plates. Because of this, manufacturing complex shapes with RHA plates raises costs.

Eventually some factories began constructing cast homogenous armour (CHA) turrets for the T-34. Some could not make CHA turrets and continued to build RHA turrets. CHA turrets came into play for the T-34 because they could be made into almost any shape desired and were less costly to produce. The latter factor was a key selling-point for the Red Army. Six factories were eventually involved in manufacturing the T-34 series.

A drawback of CHA is that it must often be thicker and therefore heavier because it lacks the durability added by the work-hardening process of manufacturing RHA. This disadvantage offset by the more rounded surfaces made possible with CHA in theory increases the chances of incoming projectiles glancing off instead of penetrating.

In the book titled *T-34 in Action: Soviet Tank Troops in WWII* one of the Red Army tankers interviewed recalled that it was much safer riding in the RHA hull of the tank than the CHA turret: 'The turret, by contrast, was pierced relatively easily, its softer cast armour provided poor resistance even to the 37mm shells of automatic AA [anti-aircraft] guns.' An early postwar US Army study concluded that the RHA hulls of M4 series medium tanks offered a higher degree of protection than those constructed of CHA.

Based on a British examination of a T-34 with a CHA turret supplied by the Soviet Union, the front of its turret was 65mm thick, not counting its round CHA gun shield (mantlet) that ranged in thickness from 25mm to 45mm. Side armour on the CHA T-34 turret turned out to be 65mm thick and sloped at 31 degrees, with the turret rear plate 47mm thick and sloped at 31 degrees.

That original T-34 CHA narrow turret design was supplemented by a much simpler and larger hexagonal-shaped CHA turret beginning in June 1942 (nicknamed 'the screw-nut' by Red Army tankers) that had two overhead hatches in the turret roof. The earlier RHA and CHA turrets of the T-34 had a single one-piece overhead hatch nicknamed 'the pie' by Red Army tankers due to its shape.

By the summer of 1943 new production examples of the hexagonal-shaped CHA turret began appearing with a vehicle commander's cupola. However, the vehicle commander still had to do double duty as the tank's gunner, leaving him little opportunity to use his cupola to improve his situational awareness in combat. Frontal armour on the hexagonal-shaped CHA turret came in at 70mm.

Throughout the series production run of the T-34, it retained the original 47mm-thick glacis sloped at 60 degrees. That slope provided it with equivalent protection of 90mm of armour. The British listed the upper side hull armour on the T-34 as 45mm thick with a 41-degree slope and the horizontal bottom hull plate as 21mm thick.

The original upper and lower front hull of the T-34 consisted of a single plate of armour bent into shape. The bending process proved difficult at the factory. It also resulted in a ballistic weak spot at the leading edge of the bow. The following appears in a US Army report on a T-34 built in 1941 and supplied by the Soviet government to the American government for evaluation: 'The bow casting of the T-34 tank was very unsound and would have been rejected under American standards.' The answer proved to be riveting (later welding) of two separate pieces of armour plate together, joined together and reinforced by a 100mm-thick armoured connecting crossbeam.

Found within a declassified CIA report titled 'Review of Soviet Ordnance Metallurgy' and dated April 1953 is the following extract on American impressions after examining knocked-out wartime Soviet tanks left behind in Central Europe:

> Although welds in Soviet tanks are inferior in quality and much more brittle than corresponding welds in American tanks, this condition has not been a major factor in impairing the battlefield performance of Soviet armor. Poor joint fits, sloppy appearance, jagged and rough finishes should not divert attention from the fact that the Soviet tanks are rugged and battleworthy and require many fewer man-hours of labor and precision machine tools, jigs, and fixtures to construct than American tanks of corresponding offensive capabilities.

Crew Issues

The T-34 suspension system had springs but lacked shock absorbers. That meant there was no damping of the tank's hull as it crossed uneven terrain and began to oscillate. Shock absorbers (dampers) reduce swaying (oscillations) by turning the generated kinetic energy into heat and preventing tanks from bottoming out their hulls when crossing rough terrain.

The lack of shock absorbers on the T-34 contributed to the crew's fatigue, worsened by the tank's inadequate ventilation system. It consisted of a single electrically-powered ventilation fan mounted in the front of the turret roof. Former Red Army tankers recall that it was not uncommon for loaders to pass out in their T-34s from the noxious fumes generated during firing of the main gun, a problem not uncommon in many Second World War tanks.

The drivers (referred to as driver/mechanics by the Red Army) of T-34s had a tough job with tractor-like steering clutches connected to an unreliable mechanical booster. Making the driver/mechanics' job even more difficult was a four-speed manual transmission, which took a great deal of effort to shift, forcing them to use a mallet or call upon the bow machine-gunner to assist. Eventually an improved five-speed transmission appeared for the T-34 series in late 1943.

We Want Something Else

The numerous unresolved issues involving both the T-34 prototypes and the early-production examples proved a significant concern to many high-ranking officials. In place of the T-34, these same officials believed in developing a brand-new tank designated the T-34M.

The T-34M's plans had originated in March 1940, with some initial design work beginning in April that year. However, it took until January 1941 before enough factory space became available to build a wooden mock-up. Plans called for two prototype T-34Ms to be ready by August 1941.

The T-34M would feature a larger three-man turret, allowing the vehicle commander to concentrate on directing his crew (or other tanks as a platoon commander) rather than doing double duty as the gunner. Another significant modification would involve replacing the T-34's Christie suspension with a torsion bar suspension system as the Christie suspension was reaching the limit of its weight-carrying capacity.

However, the Red Army soon began to have second thoughts about the T-34M and decided not to order it into production. The main reason was that it would have required massive changes to the existing production lines while not offering a significant benefit over the existing T-34s. The Red Army could not afford to potentially lose weeks of T-34 production output while setting up new production lines for the T-34M.

Leadership Failures

There were 1,225 examples of the T-34 in the Red Army inventory at the time of the German invasion in 1941. Of that number, 967 were with units in the field. In theory, the early-production T-34 had a clear advantage over its German Army medium tank counterparts in armament, armour protection and mobility. These assets, however, were offset by several factors, including the Red Army's pre-invasion shortages of everything from main gun ammunition to fuel and spare parts. These shortfalls in turn limited the training of tank and maintenance crews before the German invasion.

In a 12 July 1941 diary entry of a senior-level German general appears the following passage on the Red Army tank crews' poor level of training: 'The majority of driver-mechanics of the latest Soviet tanks in the 8th Mechanized Corps, for example, had just three to five hours' practical driving experience.'

The lack of training extended up to the senior command levels of the Red Army. The following was noted in an August 1941 Red Army report:

Tanks were thrown into the attack without any information about the disposition of the enemy's system of fire and the nature of the terrain.

> Commanders of the units and combined-arms formations gave unclear and dubious tasks to the tanks and failed to arrange air, infantry and artillery support for the tanks ... There were cases of shooting up our own tanks by friendly artillery because of the lack of coordination of artillery fire.

The inability of the Red Army leadership to master the proper employment of tanks in battle continued well into 1942, as described in the following passage from a 16 October 1942 Red Army report:

> Commanders of companies and battalions moving in front of the battle formations are not able to monitor tanks or control the battle of their sub-units, and turn into private soldiers of the tank commanders, while the units, not having control, lose their orientation and roam around the battlefield, suffering pointless losses.

Another related comment appeared in the same October 1942 report: 'As a rule, tanks do not maneuver on the battlefield, do not use the terrain for a covert approach and surprise strike on the flank and in the rear, and most often attack head-on.'

Communication Problems

A significant problem was an early-war shortage of radios; only the tanks of platoon commanders and above had radios. Everybody else depended on flag signals or flares to communicate with each other. The radios that were available compared poorly to the German radios tested. From a Red Army report dated 11 October 1940 is this passage: 'Judging by all basic characteristics, the radio sets of the German tank are superior to that installed in the domestic tank. I consider it useful to conduct the design and development of a new type of radio on the basis of the available German models.' Postwar Soviet Army radios were based on German Second World War radio designs.

The Red Army report on the trials conducted with the two T-34 prototypes between February and April 1940 mentioned the following: 'The 71-TK-3 [AM] radio set mounted in the tank doesn't satisfy requirements given for tank radio sets due to reasons of the device's large dimensions, complicated operation and the inability to tune out interference when using the radio.'

It took until 1943 before Soviet industry could build enough radios to outfit about 75 per cent of the T-34 series tanks coming off the assembly lines. However, a lack of a sufficient number of radio repairmen proved problematic throughout the war.

Compared to German AM tank radios, the early-production Red Army AM tank radios proved to be substandard due to their short effective ranges. By copying German-made radios, the quality of Red Army radios began to improve from 1943.

German Army Impressions

A German report noted that the Red Army T-34 crews were very slow in locating and engaging targets. In contrast, on average German tank crews could fire three rounds in the same time that it took Red Army tankers to fire a single round from a T-34.

In the December 1940 Red Army report on the testing of three early-production T-34s, the tank's main gun practical rate of fire was only two rounds per minute. With a revised main gun ammunition stowage arrangement that appeared in May 1941, a good loader could manage four rounds per minute.

The T-34 had an electrically-powered turret traverse mechanism with a poor reputation for reliability. It proved awkward to use, and as it did not turn the turret smoothly it made aiming the main gun difficult for the vehicle commander/gunner. Most relied on the manual rotation of the turret for the final aiming of the tank's main gun.

In a US Army wartime technical evaluation of a 1941-built T-34 provided by the Soviet government appears this passage on the tank's power traverse system: 'The electrical mechanism for rotating the turret is very bad. The motor is weak, very overloaded and sparks horribly, as a result of which the device regulating the speed of the rotation burns out and the teeth of the cogwheels break into pieces.'

The various issues that handicapped the T-34 turret crew in engaging targets appeared in an 8 March 1943 letter between high-ranking Soviet officials:

Firing on the Move

Unlike German tankers that fired from short halts when taking part in offensive operations, Red Army tankers seen in wartime newsreels often fired when on the move. From the Tank Archives blog is an extract from a translated Red Army report documenting that practice:

> Firing on the move when attacking a defending enemy should done from all weapons after the tank breaks away from our infantry. The rate of fire should be maximum without regard for hitting. In this case, undershooting is better than overshooting. Keep firing like this until the platoon or even the whole formation enters enemy lines, then finish off strongholds with precise fire.

'The awkward mutual arrangement of the turret's traversing mechanism and the sight, which makes aiming the gun at a target difficult ... the low speed of the turret's traverse [manually] and the need to apply strong forces to turn it, especially on slopes.'

T-34 Powertrain

The diesel engine proved to be an essential element of the T-34's design and capabilities. There were, however, reliability and durability problems early on with the engines. In a late 1942 Red Army report are the following findings on T-34s recovered from battlefields: 'Around 35 per cent of tanks examined in the relevant subset were disabled through internal mechanical failure without any armor damage, primarily through failure of the engine. This indicates a need to improve the quality of engine construction and the design of engines with longer service lives.'

The engines on the early-production T-34s were not the only issues affecting their mobility. The problems extended to their transmissions and suspension systems. These issues came about due to poor quality control at the factories that built T-34 tanks. The cause was dependence on a largely unskilled labour pool (including women, children and older men no longer fit for military service) labouring under substandard conditions. The horrendous working conditions at the tank factories, including a lack of food, resulted in a personnel turnover rate of up to 25 per cent, with more than half those workers fleeing from the factory grounds or their barracks to return home.

The disruption caused by the forced relocation of Soviet tank factories to areas beyond the reach of the German military between August and December 1941 undoubtedly contributed to the T-34's quality control problems.

Even without the early-production T-34 quality control problems, the tank's transmission and those in the KV-series heavy tanks proved problematic. The following example appears in a memo written to Stalin by a high-ranking Red Army officer on 16 May 1942:

> The obsolescence and primitiveness of our design approaches in the realm of designing transmissions leads in the final analysis to a sharp reduction in the number of vehicles that can take part in combat; the vehicles all too often are not so much being used, as being tinkered with and repaired without any sort of damage from enemy fire ... In short, in the light of the present-day designs of Allied and captured German tanks, the conservatism and obsolescence of design thought in the realm of tank transmissions is indisputable.

In the book *Tank Power of the USSR* by Mikhail Svirin is the following passage: 'It should be noted that the quality of the assembly of domestic armored fighting vehicles was in some cases unsatisfactory, which significantly shortened their service lives and contributed to the high loss of personnel in the 1942–1943 period.'

A translated German Army report from June 1944 that appears in 'Panzer tracts no. 19-2: *Beute-panzerkampfwagen*' by Thomas Jentz and Werner Regenberg mentions the issues encountered by a rear area security unit when trying to employ captured T-34s:

> Regardless of our limited experience, it can be stated that the Russian tanks are not suitable for long road marches and high speeds … Difficulties and breakdowns of the steering clutches have occurred with all the new *Beute* [captured] -*Panzer*. In difficult terrain, on the march, and during the attack, in which the Panzer must be frequently steered and turned, within a short time the steering clutches overheat and are coated with oil. The result is that the clutches don't grip and the Panzer is no longer maneuverable. After they have cooled, the clutches must be rinsed with a lot of fuel.

In a US Army evaluation of a T-34 built in 1941 supplied by the Soviet government to the American government in late 1942, appears the following passage:

> Despite the advantages of the use of diesel, the good contours of the tanks, thick armor, good and reliable armaments, the successful design of the tracks, etc., Russian tanks are significantly inferior to American tanks in their simplicity of driving, maneuverability, the strength of firing (a reference to muzzle velocity), speed, the reliability of mechanical construction and the ease of keeping them running.

Diesel Pros and Cons

Diesel engines offered improved thermal efficiency, which generated a greater range per gallon compared to their gasoline-powered counterparts. Diesel engines also deliver more torque at low engine speeds than gasoline engines, requiring fewer gear changes and less complex transmissions.

A critical human safety factor in favour of diesel engines for combat vehicles is its lower propensity to burn at the same temperature and pressure as gasoline. With the T-34, that advantage was offset by having four of its fuel tanks located within the vehicle's hull fighting compartment.

In the American M4 series tanks, all the fuel tanks resided in the engine compartment, separated from the fighting compartment by a firewall, the same arrangement as in the Panzer III. On the Panzer IV, the fuel tanks were inside the hull but at the bottom, with an armoured plate on top that separated them from the fighting compartment.

When an enemy projectile of sufficient calibre containing a high-explosive (HE) filler detonated within the T-34 fighting compartment, diesel fumes in near-empty fuel tanks quickly reached their flashpoint and the required pressure and ignited. One source cites a figure of 25 per cent of T-34s burning when penetrated. In addition, the unprotected main gun rounds in the fighting compartment would typically detonate or at least burn, destroying the tank and killing most if not all the crew.

In the book titled *T-34 in Action: Soviet Tank Troops in WWII* appears a passage by a non-Red Army tanker on his thoughts regarding his tanker counterparts:

> I had a special sympathy towards tankmen ... they suffered such awful deaths. If a tank was knocked out, and they often were, it meant almost certain death: one or two men could bail out, but not more ... The most awful thing was the burns they had. In those days, burns of 40 percent of the skin area were lethal.

Of the approximately 400,000 tankers the Red Army put into the field during the Second World War, around 300,000 would perish.

Other Issues Affecting the T-34

Making matters worse on the battlefield, the uneducated rural manpower that often manned the Red Army's tanks had little or no experience of operating complex machinery. Despite the general simplicity of operation of the T-34 tank series, it still proved to be a daunting task for many Red Army tankers to master its use in combat and its maintenance requirements.

The lack of knowledge about the workings of modern military machinery – be it tanks, aircraft or artillery – extended up into the most senior levels of the Red Army. Red Army general, later Marshal Georgy K. Zhukov stated that many of his senior wartime counterparts were 'technologically illiterate'.

Some of the Red Army senior leadership was well aware of the T-34's design limitations, factory quality control issues and the poor level of mechanical knowledge among its tankers. However, the realization that the majority of T-34 tanks and their crews seldom survived long enough for the shortfalls of the vehicle's mechanical components to become a concern made those problems a somewhat moot point.

Stalin, on the other hand, in his mind felt that there were other forces at work contributing to the poor early showing of the Red Army's armour branch, as seen in this directive dated 10 August 1942:

> Our tank units and formations often suffer greater losses through mechanical breakdowns than they do in battle ... Since such a high incidence of mechanical defects is implausible, the Supreme High Command sees in it covert sabotage and wrecking on the part of certain tank crews who try to exploit small mechanical problems to leave their tanks on the battlefield and avoid battle.

In November 1943 the Red Army supplied a T-34 with a CHA turret to the British Army for technical evaluation. In a document titled 'Preliminary Report No. 20: Russian T-34' dated February 1944, the British noted the rough finish on much of the vehicle. However, they also made mention of the added work to those parts and components crucial to the tank's functioning:

> When necessary, for efficient functioning, for example, in the periscopic dial sight, the fuel pump, and certain engine components, an excellent finish is

attained, but where not essential, it is often rough. No military or mechanical advantage appears to be sacrificed thereby, but a more fully developed industry might be expected to show more refinement without necessarily expending more man-hours.

Main Gun Round Problems

Despite implementing the F-34 main gun on the T-34 Model 1941, Red Army tank crews could still not take advantage of its theoretical capabilities. The armour-piercing (AP) ammunition and fuses were of poor quality and in short supply due to manufacturing problems and a lack of high-quality alloy steel.

On 9 July 1941 a high-ranking Red Army officer ordered that T-34 vehicle commanders/gunners aim at the tracks of enemy tanks with other types of rounds, such as high-explosive (HE), when short of AP rounds.

In a July 1945 Red Army document, a senior officer stated: 'As is known, the domestic armor-piercing shells with respect to their quality proved somewhat worse than the quality of armor-piercing shells of the Allied armies and of the enemy's army.'

Despite these problems, the available AP rounds could still penetrate the original armour configuration of the German Panzer III and Panzer IV medium tanks in the summer and autumn of 1941. German reports mention that their front hulls suffered penetrations, and vehicle commander cupolas were ripped off turret roofs.

Design Issues

In general, Soviet industry proved unable to build long-lasting, reliable tracks. Those on the T-34 series were supposed to last about 1,900 miles, but seldom survived for more than 600 miles. One Red Army engineer noted in a March 1941 report that some tank tracks began to fail after only eight to ten hours of use. The quality of Soviet industry-made tracks started to improve in 1943.

From a 1942 Red Army report is the following passage on problems with the T-34's suspension and tracks:

> The Christie's suspension was tested a long time ago by the Americans and unconditionally rejected. On our tanks, as a result of the poor steel on the springs, it very quickly fatigues, and as a result, clearance is noticeably reduced. The deficiencies in our tracks from their viewpoint result from the lightness of their construction. They can easily be damaged by small-caliber and mortar rounds. The pins are extremely poorly tempered and made of poor steel. As a result, they quickly wear, and the track often breaks.

A Universal Tank

The Soviet military organization that oversaw tank development for the Red Army put forth a requirement in June 1942 calling for a universal tank. It was to replace both the T-34 series and the KV heavy tank series. What arose from that requirement became the T-43, with the prototype appearing in March 1943. The new tank incorporated many parts and components from the T-34 series, including its 76.2mm main gun.

Like the cancelled T-34M, the T-43 featured torsion bar suspension and a larger turret that included a cupola for the vehicle commander. It differed from both the T-34 and the T-34M in the thickness of its armour, although still not enough to protect it from German 88mm guns.

Testing also showed that the thicker armour of the T-34M which increased the vehicle weight significantly decreased mobility compared to the T-34. That, and the fact that the 76.2mm main gun was inadequate in dealing with better-armoured German tanks appearing in the summer of 1943, led to the end of work on the T-43.

Combat Losses

Approximately 2,300 T-34s were lost to combat and non-combat causes from June to December 1941. Around 50 per cent of those knocked out in action through to September 1942 were accounted for by the 50mm main gun on the Panzer III medium tank and its towed anti-tank version.

The German 37mm towed anti-tank gun and the 37mm main gun on some Panzer III medium tanks each accounted for approximately 10 per cent of T-34 combat losses.

In theory, T-34 armour was proof against 37mm anti-tank projectiles. T-34s drove through a hail of 37mm anti-tank gunfire in many encounters with German forces without suffering any disabling penetrations. However, poor quality welding of some early-production T-34 hulls and turrets resulted in weak spots at weld joints that left the tanks vulnerable to smaller-calibre anti-tank projectiles.

An example of smaller-calibre rounds penetrating the T-34 armour appears in a report dated 2 August 1941 from the Red Army 10th Tank Division: 'Hull armor is penetrated at 300 to 400 meters [328 to 437 yards] by a 37mm antitank round. Side armor is penetrated by a 20mm antitank round ... With a direct hit by a shell, the driver's front hatch collapses.'

The T-34's 47mm thick glacis sloped at 60 degrees proved very effective in stopping German 50mm AP rounds. Out of a total of 109 hits, 89 per cent failed to penetrate. When striking the 40-degree sloped upper hull side plates, only 25 per cent of 50mm AP projectiles penetrated.

In a May 1942 German Army report appears this extract: 'Combating the T-34 with the 5cm [50mm] KwK tank gun is possible only at short ranges from the flank or rear, where it is important to achieve a hit as perpendicular to the surface as possible.'

In a German Army report dated June 1943 appears another passage on their 50mm tank gun's ineffectiveness:

Half a dozen anti-tank guns fire shells at him [a T-34], which sounds like a drumroll. But he drives staunchly through our line like an impregnable

Evaluating T-34 Tank Losses

Armies evaluate losses and damage to weapons to identify ways to avoid losses, which otherwise deplete forces, consume repair resources and require new crewmen, etc.

In a 1942 Red Army report, they reviewed damage to 178 T-34 series tanks moved to rear area repair depots during September–October. It found, for example, that 35 per cent had mechanical issues, while armour penetrations had disabled the other 65 per cent.

Of those suffering armour penetrations, 81 per cent of the projectile impacts were on the hull and only 19 per cent on the turret. Of the projectile strikes on the hull, half hit the hull sides and 22 per cent the glacis. Of those strikes on the hull sides, the highest rate of penetrations occurred against the vertical side armour between the tank's road wheels.

The report noted that both the vertical and sloped armour of T-34 tanks suffered a similar number of strikes, with 23 per cent on vertical surfaces and 27.5 per cent on sloped surfaces. However, there is a significant disparity when analyzing the penetrations of these surfaces. Of penetrations, 33.9 per cent occurred on vertical armour and 17.25 per cent on sloped armour. On average, the T-34's exposed vertical side armour around its road wheels was penetrated twice as often as the sloped side hull armour above the vehicle's road wheels.

Of the T-34 tanks reviewed, their upper glacis received only 20 per cent of all impacts and just 8.2 per cent of all penetrations. Therefore, the report's authors concluded that vehicle commanders failed to assess the risk of a particular path when on the attack, thus exposing their thinner hull flanks.

prehistoric monster ... It is remarkable that Lieutenant Steup's tank made hits on a T-34, once at about 20 metres [22 yards] and four times at 50 metres [55 yards], with *Panzergranate* 40 [calibre 5cm], without any noticeable effect.

The Odds Got Worse

During the summer of 1943, losses among T-34 series tanks rose due to a new generation of German anti-tank weapons appearing. Around 40 per cent of losses were to 75mm guns, whether they were towed or vehicle-mounted, with 88mm guns inflicting another 26 per cent of the combat losses. Reflecting the German introduction of larger and more powerful anti-tank guns, 87 to 99 per cent of all AP projectile strikes on T-34s resulted in penetration. The Red Army lost around 14,000 T-34s in 1943.

Within a US Department of the Army pamphlet dated November 1950 titled 'Russian Combat Methods in World War II' is a passage on an encounter between the German Army (reported by a senior German officer) and the Red Army that took place in August 1943, which demonstrates what T-34 crews were up against:

During the morning, Red tanks had worked their way forward in the hollows up to the southern edges of the cornfields. Then they made a mass dash across the road in full sight. The leading waves of Russian T34s were caught in the fierce defensive fire of the Panthers and were on fire before they could reach the main line of resistance. But wave after wave followed until they flowed across in the protecting hollows and pushed forward into the battle position. Here they were trapped in the net of anti-tank and anti-aircraft guns, Hornets (88mm tank destroyers) and Wasps (self-propelled 105mm light field howitzers) ... and large numbers of them put out of action.

The last waves were still attempting to force a breakthrough in concentrated masses when they were attacked by Tigers and self-propelled assault guns ... The price they paid for this mass tank assault amounted to 184 knocked-out T34s.

T-34 First-Generation Summary

By the time production of the Model 1943 ended in 1944, approximately 35,000 examples of T-34 series tanks armed with the 76.2mm main gun had come out of the factories. The following list is a production breakdown based on Russian online history databases by year: 1940 (115), 1941 (2,996), 1942 (12,520), 1943 (15,696), and 1944 (3,986). The number of T-34s built reflects the statement attributed to Stalin that 'quantity has a quality all its own.' In comparison, German industry made only 5,774 examples of the Panzer III and 8,553 examples of the Panzer IV between 1937 and 1945.

A British Army document labelled 'Preliminary Report No. 20: Russian T-34' and dated February 1944 appears as an extract:

When it is considered how recently Russia has become industrialized and how great a proportion of the industrial regions have been overrun by the enemy with the consequent loss or hurried evacuation of plant and workers, the design and production of such useful tanks in such great numbers stands out as an engineering achievement of the first magnitude.

We Need a Bigger Gun

It took the German introduction of the Panther during Operation CITADEL (4–16 July 1943) and the appearance of more Tiger heavy tanks for Stalin and the Red Army leadership to realize just how obsolete the T-34 had become. The solution to the problem was up-gunning the T-34 with an 85mm main gun based on a prewar design for an anti-aircraft gun.

The Red Army tasked different design teams for a suitable 85mm gun. Two appeared in short order, receiving the initial designations of D-5 and S-53. The D-5 was already in use on other tanks and a self-propelled gun/tank destroyer. However, due to political favouritism, the S-53 gun became the preferred choice.

We Need a New Turret

Testing quickly revealed that the S-53 gun was too large to fit into the turret of a T-34 tank, hence the call for a new larger turret with a wider turret ring came about. In November 1943, two S-53 guns went into new turrets based on the design from the cancelled T-43 tank. These up-gunned turrets then went onto the chassis of modified T-34s and received the factory designation Obiekt 135.

Testing the two Obiekt 135 prototypes proved so promising that Stalin and senior officials overseeing tank designs approved it for Red Army service on 15 December 1943 as the T-34-85, even before testing finished. Stalin wanted the T-34-85 ready for full-scale production by February 1944. The larger and heavier turret brought the T-34-85's weight up to around 36 tons.

A Stopgap

A design problem discovered in December 1943 concerning the recoil system of the S-53 gun put an abrupt halt to its production. As an interim measure, the Red Army decided that the D-5 version of the 85mm gun should be fitted into the T-34-85 to meet Stalin's deadline. To reflect its modification to fit inside a tank, the suffix letter 'T' was added to the D-5 designation.

The initial production batch of around 800 examples of the T-34-85 with the D-5T main gun retained the four-man crew of the 76.2mm gun-armed T-34s, with the vehicle commander still doubling as the gunner. They began showing up with field units starting in March 1944.

Another Version of the 85mm Gun

A superior and lighter 85mm gun labelled the ZIS-S-53 began appearing on the T-34-85 production lines in early 1944. A Finnish Army report dated 1944 considered the ZIS-S-53 85mm main gun on the T-34-85 comparable to the German 88mm gun in operational parameters, only coming up short in range and trajectory to its German counterpart due to the inferior quality of Soviet industry propellant. The same Finnish Army report also noted that the armour on the T-34-85 proved superior to that found on the T-34.

Those T-34-85 tanks armed with the ZIS-S-53 85mm main gun featured other improvements over the early-production examples armed with the D-5T 85mm main gun. The most important was the addition of a fifth crewman assigned as the gunner, freeing the vehicle commander from that job. The vehicle commander's cupola and the two electrically-powered ventilation blowers were moved rearward on the turret roof to make room for the gunner, a readily apparent design feature to distinguish late-production T-34-85 tanks armed with the ZIS-S-53 85mm main gun from the early-production T-34-85s armed with the D-5T 85mm main gun.

Other changes in the interior configuration of the T-34-85 tanks armed with the ZIS-S-53 85mm main gun included the relocation of the front hull-mounted radio into the vehicle's turret bustle. An external identifying feature of this change is the radio's antenna moving from the right-hand side of the front hull to a position on the turret roof next to the vehicle commander's cupola.

Early-production T-34-85s made do without a powered turret traverse mechanism. However, an electrically-powered mechanism soon appeared. The tanks so fitted had a slight bulge in the turret wall armour opposite the gunner's position in the turret to make room for it.

A declassified CIA report titled 'Engineering Analysis of the Russian T-34-85 Tank' dated September 1951 had the following to say about the armour protection of a vehicle built in 1945 and captured by the US Army during the Korean War: 'The T-34 armor had impact strength greater than required by US Army specification yet exceeded our specification in hardness by as much as 100 points Brinell. This armor should have excellent penetrating resistance (for a given thickness) but might have been expected to spall.'

Summing Up

The fielding of the T-34-85 did much to improve Red Army tankers' morale, as seen in the following passage:

> In essence, until we got the 85mm gun, we had to run from Tigers like rabbits and look for an opportunity to turn back and get at their flanks. It was difficult. If you saw a Tiger 800 to 1,000 meters [875 to 1,094 yards] away and it started crossing you, while it moved its gun horizontally, you could stay in your tank, but once it started moving vertically, you'd better jump out or you could get burned! It never happened to me, but other guys bailed out. But when the T-34-85 entered service, we could stand up against enemy tanks one by one.

Despite the bravado of some Red Army tankers and occasional successes, the reality is that the T-34-85 still could not compare to the Panther or Tiger. They could, however, more capably deal with the latest models of the more numerous Panzer IV medium tanks and the various specialized and improvised tank destroyers fielded by the late-war German Army.

A total of 11,050 examples of the T-34-85 came off the assembly lines during 1944, with another 7,430 units by May 1945. The large numbers built helped to offset those lost in action. Approximately 16,900 Red Army tanks of all types were lost in 1944, mostly T-34-85s, and another 8,700 in 1945, again primarily T-34-85s.

To the Red Army, the tactical superiority of some German tanks meant little in the big picture of the war. It saw the T-34 and the T-34-85 as operational and strategic weapons intended to win wars, not individual engagements, hence the continued emphasis on numbers, and there simply weren't enough German Tigers and Panthers to counter them.

As testament to the design and capability of the T-34-85, it was made postwar by Czech and Polish factories in the newly-occupied Eastern Europe and was given to dozens of countries by the Soviet Union for military aid. It can still be found in conflict zones today.

T-44 Medium Tank

The last wartime Red Army medium tank design received the designation T-44. The tank's designers were influenced by the lessons learned from the wartime shortcomings of the T-34-85. However, the three-man turret of the new 35-ton medium tank proved to be very similar to its predecessor, including its 85mm main gun.

It was the chassis design that marked the T-44 as the next big step in tank design. The tank's low-slung hull was wider and shorter than the T-34, reducing its profile, and was more thickly armoured. These design changes became possible by eliminating the bow gunner's position and mounting the diesel engine in the rear hull transversely rather than inline as on the T-34. The T-44 also came with a torsion bar suspension system.

An advantage with the T-44 chassis design was that the turret sat much closer to the centre of the tank's hull, rather than forward as on the T-34 series. The centre-mounting of the turret reduced the oscillation imparted to the main gun during operation and allowed for a significant increase in accuracy when firing on the move. It also helped even out the load on the suspension system. On the T-34-85 the forward suspension system was under a great deal more load than the rear due to the heavy forward-mounted turret.

Despite breaking ground with the chassis design, the T-44 had some issues, especially its powertrain and chiefly its new transmission. The engine was an improved model from the version that powered the T-34. Due to retaining the turret layout of the T-34-85, it could not fit a larger main gun, much desired by the Red Army, which had been pushing for a 100mm main gun.

Despite the design missteps with the T-44, the Red Army authorized its production. A total of 1,823 examples came down the assembly lines between November 1944 and 1947. The Red Army did not commit any wartime-built T-44s to combat. However, the design laid the groundwork for follow-on Cold War-era T-54 and T-55 series medium tanks.

The first medium tanks in the Red Army were the British-designed and built Mark A Whippets, an example of which is pictured here. The tank initially saw combat with the British Army in the last year of the First World War. Following that conflict, the British government supplied a number of Whippets to anti-Bolshevik forces engaged in the Russian Civil War (November 1917 to October 1922). With the eventual Bolshevik (Communist) victory, they came under the control of the Red Army. (*Dreamstime*)

(**Above**) In 1931 the Red Army bought fifteen examples of the British-designed and built Vickers Mark II medium tank (pictured here) for evaluation. It had a five-man crew and proved to be the first tank designed to take three men in its turret. The Vickers Mark II entered British Army service in 1926 and was retired in 1939. Armament consisted of a 47mm main gun and three machine guns. The Red Army proved to be unimpressed by the Mark II and never sought to copy the design for its own use. (*PICRYL*)

(**Opposite, above**) The first Soviet-designed Red Army tank was the six-man T-28 medium tank pictured here. It sported three turrets. The uppermost had 360 degrees of traverse and was armed with a short-barrelled 76.2mm main gun. Two smaller one-man turrets in front of and below the larger elevated main turret had only a single machine gun each and also had only limited traverse. The front of the uppermost turret on the T-28 featured 30mm thick armour. (*Dreamstime*)

(**Opposite, below**) A Red Army motorcycle messenger is shown here handing orders to the vehicle commander of a T-28 medium tank. Instead having of a coaxial machine gun mounted to fire alongside the 76.2mm main gun, the T-28 had a separate ball mount for a 7.62mm machine gun mounted on the right side of the turret. A total of 508 examples of the T-28 came off the assembly lines between 1934 and 1940. Their combat debut was in the First Russo-Finnish War (November 1939 to March 1940), during which they proved badly under-armoured when confronted by Finnish Army towed anti-tank guns. (*Author's collection*)

(**Above**) Following the T-28 medium tank into Red Army service was the T-34 medium tank in September 1940. The T-34 pictured here was an early-production example armed with a low-velocity L-11 76.2mm main gun. Note the oddly-contoured cast homogenous armour (CHA) gun-shield specific to T-34s fitted with the L-11 7.62mm gun. The L-11 was a stand-in until delivery of the more potent 76.2mm gun designated the F-34. The F-34 first showed up on new-production T-34s in February 1941. (*Dreamstime*)

(**Above**) Some design features on the T-34 pictured here identify it as an early-production vehicle. These include the rolled homogenous armour (RHA) turret, the driver's hatch with a single forward-facing periscope and the glacis plate bolted to the lower front hull plate. T-34s armed with the F-34 76.2mm main gun as seen here have a different gun shield design to those armed with the L-11 76.2mm main gun. (*Pierre-Olivier Buan*)

(**Opposite, below**) The majority of road wheels fitted to the four-man T-34s were rubber-rimmed. When a temporary shortage of rubber occurred, some factories began fitting new-production T-34s with all-steel road wheels as seen on the vehicle pictured here. Also visible in this image are the two towing shackles on the lower glacis and the later-production driver's hatch with two forward-facing periscopes. The early-production T-34 weighed in at about 29 tons. It had a length of about 22ft, a width of around 10ft and a height of 8ft. (*Dreamstime*)

(**Above**) All T-34s came with an RHA welded hull as seen in this image. This vehicle has a mixture of road wheels, including the original rubber-rimmed concave type, the later-production spoked rubber-rimmed road wheels and the stopgap all-steel version. On the rear hull are two small armoured housings which protect a portion of the engine's exhaust pipes. The T-34's diesel engine lacked mufflers, hence the complaints from Red Army tankers that their loud T-34s warned the enemy of their presence. (*Pierre-Olivier Buan*)

(**Opposite, above**) In this image we are looking into an early-production T-34's RHA turret from the underside. Attached to the underside of the gun's cradle are steel weights to aid in balancing the 76.2mm main gun in its trunnions. Trunnions allow the gun to be elevated and depressed and also pass recoil forces onto the weapon's cradle when fired. Note the leather pads attached at intervals to the interior turret ring behind the vehicle commander's and loader's positions. (*SA-Kuva*)

(**Opposite, below**) The early-production T-34 turrets constructed of RHA plate were time-consuming and difficult to make. Soviet industry eventually switched to making cast homogenous armour (CHA) turrets, such as the example pictured here. CHA lends itself well to the construction of complex shapes such as tank turrets and gun shields. Such casting is also a less complicated and time-consuming process, hence is also more cost-effective. These were all essential attributes as the Red Army wanted as many T-34s as possible built in the shortest amount of time. (*Dreamstime*)

(**Opposite, above**) An early-production T-34 fitted with a CHA turret armed with an L-11 76.2mm main gun. The front hull-mounted machine gun proved of limited usefulness as it offered poor visibility for sighting targets and so posed a danger to friendly infantry-men in the heat of battle. With widespread late-war German introduction of shaped-charge infantry anti-tank weapons, a bow-mounted machine gun became more valuable. (*Dreamstime*)

(**Opposite, below**) There was an advantage in having the T-34's transmission located in the vehicle's rear hull. It allowed the designers to make the T-34 much lower than other medium tanks of the day with front hull-mounted transmissions. That advantage is evident in this image of a first-generation M4 series tank pictured alongside a mid-production CHA turreted T-34. The small turret and well-sloped glacis and upper hull sides of the latter provided a much higher level of protection than the American tank's hull and turret's vertical sides. (*Author's collection*)

(**Above**) In this photograph of an RHA turret-equipped T-34, we see the large one-piece hatch that Red Army tankers nicknamed 'the pie'. It provides room during repairs to remove the main gun's cradle and the four fuel tanks in the lower hull fighting compartment. The gun itself came out of the rear of the turret. German tank main guns came out of the front of the turret, making their removal a bit easier. (*Pierre-Olivier Buan*)

(**Above**) In this photograph taken during a demonstration of historical Red Army tanks, we see the overhead hatch on a CHA turret-equipped T-34. As can be imagined, the large and heavy one-piece hatch proved unpopular with the turret crews of T-34s. It was clear to all that it would hinder escape from their vehicle if struck by a disabling enemy round, especially if the turret crewmen were wounded. (*Dreamstime*)

(**Opposite, above**) Despite the Red Army's senior leadership's aversion to making any major changes to the T-34's design as keeping production numbers as high as possible was a priority, it eventually became clear that the narrow RHA and CHA turrets were hindering tank crews' combat effectiveness. That finding led Soviet industry to design a new larger CHA hexagonal-shaped turret as seen here. Despite the roomier interior, the turret was still crewed by only two men. The vehicle commander still doubled as the tank's gunner. (*Author's collection*)

(**Below**) In addition to the new CHA hexagonal T-34 turret being larger than its narrower predecessors, it improved access with two smaller hatches instead of a single large hatch. These hatches first appeared on new-production T-34s in January 1942 at a single factory. Positive feedback on the new turret configuration led other factories to adopt the design, with at least one factory unable to switch over until mid-1943. (*Chris Hughes*)

(**Opposite, above**) The new CHA hexagonal T-34 turret came with a unique rounded CHA gun shield as seen on the vehicle pictured here. However, it retained the box-like RHA bolted armour housing, also visible, that enclosed a portion of the 76.2mm main gun's recoil cylinders. The small upright cylinder-like device on the turret roof is the vehicle commander's periscope sight. With its electrically-powered turret traverse motor, the tank's turret could be rotated 360 degrees in twelve seconds. (*Dreamstime*)

(**Opposite, below**) Looking forward from the turret bustle of an early-production T-34, we see the 76.2mm F-34 main gun's breech. To the right of the main gun's breech is a drum magazine for the coaxial 7.62mm machine gun. The tank had authorized storage for thirty-five drum magazines, each containing sixty-five rounds. Half the magazines were stored in the rear turret bustle and the other half in the forward hull. On the left-hand side of the main gun breech is the vehicle commander/gunner's optical sight. (*Author's collection*)

(**Above**) Looking in through an early T-34's open driver's hatch, the vehicle commander/ gunner's seat is seen on the right-hand side and the loader's seat on the left. In the background (with the firewall panel between engine and crew compartments removed) is the rear hull engine compartment. The vehicle had authorized stowage for seventy-seven main gun rounds, with sixty-eight stored on the fighting compartment floor in eight unarmoured bins under removable rubberized matting. On the loader's side, there are three stored main rounds on the wall and six on the vehicle commander/gunner's side. (*Author's collection*)

(**Above**) A photograph from the bottom of the fighting compartment of a T-34 looking forward. Visible is the driver's seat on the left-hand side and the front edge of the bow machine-gunner/radioman's seat on the right. The tank's radio is visible on the radioman's right. Note that the 7.62mm machine gun is absent, but the black clamp that holds it in the ball mount is visible. An escape hatch is on the hull floor in front of the bow gunner/radioman's seat. (*Chris Hughes*)

(**Above**) In imitation of German medium tanks that featured a vehicle commander cupola, new-production CHA hexagonal-shaped turrets of T-34s eventually began appearing with cupolas as seen on the tank pictured here. However, those tanks so fitted retained the two-man turret crew layout, so how much use the vehicle commander/ gunner could actually make of it in battle is unclear. (*Dreamstime*)

(**Opposite, below**) On display here is an example of one of about 2,600 examples built of a late-production T-34 with a CHA turret made using a large hydraulic press. Its use is evident from the turret's very rounded contours. Only a single factory employed this method of construction. The commander's cupola can just be seen, along with the peri-scope sights for the vehicle commander/gunner and the loader. (*Dreamstime*)

(**Above**) Combat experience in the summer of 1943 demonstrated that the 76.2mm F-34 main gun was obsolete due to its lack of penetrative capabilities. The answer was a new version of the T-34 armed with an 85mm main gun in a larger turret labelled the T-34-85. The 85mm gun on the first 500 or so examples of the new tank bore the designation D-5 or D-5T and came with a distinctive gun shield as pictured here, with four large bolts arrayed around its thick armoured collar. (*Author's collection*)

(**Opposite, above**) In March 1944 there appeared on T-34-85 assembly lines a new and improved 85mm gun labelled the ZiS-S-53. Those turrets armed with the new 85mm main gun had a different gun shield configuration as seen here, with the four bolts that held the barrel in place moved from the armoured collar to the curved gun shield. Visible on the gun shield is the small opening for the 7.62mm coaxial machine-gun barrel. (*Dreamstime*)

(**Opposite, below**) The turret bustle of the T-34-85 was much larger than that of the T-34 and provided authorized storage for sixteen main gun rounds. Another four were clipped on the interior turret wall next to the gunner. The majority of the tank main gun rounds (which varied from fifty-five to sixty) were stored in six unarmoured bins on the fighting compartment hull floor, covered by a removable rubberized mat. Like the earlier T-34, the T-34-85 did not have a turret basket. (*Dreamstime*)

(**Above**) Those T-34-85s armed with the D-5/D-5T gun retained the two-man turret crew configuration of the T-34. The T-34-85s armed with the ZiS-S-53 gun, as pictured here, had a three-man turret crew, now including a gunner. The vehicle commander's seat moved rearward to make room for the gunner. That led in turn to relocation of the vehicle commander's cupola by some 16in towards the turret roof's rear. Note the two armoured dome covers for the uppermost portion of the vehicle's ventilation fans. (*Dreamstime*)

(**Opposite, above**) The T-34-85's larger turret ring resulted in a requirement for a new T-34 chassis that could accommodate the new turret. Soviet industry used this opportunity to change the configuration of the front hull. Instead of the glacis attaching to the lower front hull with a rounded shape, the glacis was joined to the lower front hull in a simpler sharp wedge design as seen in this photograph. (*Dreamstime*)

(**Opposite, below**) Never say never: an unknown number of T-34-85 turrets were fitted onto a rebuilt earlier T-34 chassis, indicated by the rounded lower front hull of the vehicle pictured here. Earlier-production T-34-85s retained the curved front fenders of the T-34, eventually replaced by squared fenders on later-production examples. Maximum armour thickness on the front of the T-34-85 turret was about 90mm according to some sources. (*Author's collection*)

A close-up view of the gunner's position on a T-34-85. In the right foreground is the gunner's folded-up leather seat. Also visible is the gunner's TSh-16 articulated sighting telescope and his overhead periscope to the upper left of the leather brow piece. The manual turret-traverse handle is on the left side of the picture, and the gun elevation handle to its right and below. (*Chris Hughes*)

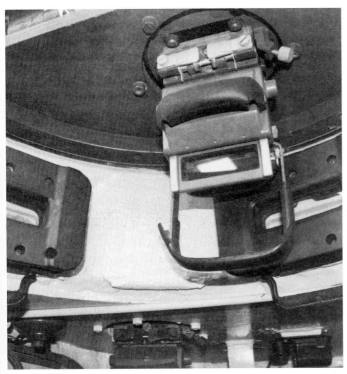

Looking up from the vehicle commander's seat in a T-34-85, one can see the interior of his cupola with two of the direct vision blocks protected by laminated glass and surrounded by rubber padding. In the approximate overhead centre of the image is the vehicle commander's 360-degree traversable periscope. The early-production cupolas had a two-piece overhead hatch, with later-production cupolas as pictured here having a one-piece overhead hatch. (*Chris Hughes*)

Visible in this cutaway T-34-85 turret is the breech of the 85mm main gun and one of the two eight-round ammunition racks located in the vehicle's turret bustle. Missing from this turret is the radio that on later-production examples was mounted to the right of the vehicle commander's upper fold-up seat. Visible are the gunner's and loader's overhead 360-degree traversable periscopes. (*Pierre-Olivier Buan*)

A line-up of 85mm main gun rounds. On the far left is the standard high-explosive (HE) fragmentation round designated the 0-365 and employed against non-armoured targets. The centre round is the standard BR-365 armour-piercing (AP) round, and the shell on the far right is the less common BR-365P round that had a tungsten carbide core for greater penetration. The suffix letter 'P' stands for 'sub-calibre' in the Russian language. It could penetrate the glacis of a Panther tank at 547 yards. (*Author's collection*)

Even before the Second World War, the Red Army senior leadership identified a requirement for an armoured personnel carrier (APC). However, Soviet industry's priority was to build as many tanks as possible before and during the Second World War. Hence designing, developing and manufacturing a suitable APC was never a priority. The alternative was having Red Army infantrymen ride into combat on the tanks as portrayed here by re-enactors. (*Dreamstime*)

Unlike the often-unreliable engines and transmissions that plagued early-production T-34s, the T-34-85s, as seen here, proved to be much more durable. Not seen on this museum vehicle are the smoke canisters that eventually appeared on the rear engine plate of T-34-85s. The original intercom system on early T-34s often failed, forcing crews to kick each other and use hand signals to communicate. On the T-34-85 the intercom system proved very reliable. (*Dreamstime*)

The planned wartime replacement for the T-34-85 was to have been the T-44 medium tank pictured here. The latter's hull design was more compact and thickly-armoured than its predecessor. However, the Red Army senior leadership felt that the turret and its 85mm main gun were not much of an improvement. Due to serious teething problems, only a few hundred T-44s came off the production lines before the end of the Second World War and were never committed to combat. (*Dreamstime*)

Chapter Four

Heavy Tanks

The first heavy tanks in Red Army service were British-designed and built Mark V heavy tanks captured from the White Army during the Russian Civil War. The British government had supplied the anti-Bolshevik forces with seventy examples of the Mark V following the First World War.

The approximately 32-ton vehicles had a crew of eight men and were armed with either machine guns or cannons. The Mark V initially saw combat during the First World War in 1918 with the British Army. The maximum armour thickness on the front hull was 16mm.

With the Red Army, the Mark V would see minor combat during the Russian Civil War against their last owners, the anti-Bolshevik armies. They survived in Red Army service through the 1920s, when the lack of spare parts ended their military careers.

The Inspiration

In 1926 British industry came up with a single example of a 35-ton heavy tank for the British Army's consideration labelled the Vickers A1E1 Independent. The eight-man, gasoline-engine-powered vehicle featured an elevated two-man turret capable of 360 degrees of traverse and armed with a 3-pounder (47mm) main gun. It also had four smaller machine gun-armed sub-turrets arrayed around and below the elevated main gun turret, each with a more limited traverse.

Armour on the Vickers A1E1 Independent topped out at 28mm. In the end, the British Army never adopted the vehicle. It had, however, sparked a great deal of interest among the Soviet officials looking for tank designs that their industry could modify and build.

The Soviets offered to buy the design plans for the Vickers A1E1 Independent, but they were rejected. They resorted to espionage and successfully acquired the information they needed.

Soviet industry began developing both a multi-turreted medium tank and a heavy tank based on the A1E1's design. Large multi-turreted tanks were popular among armies in that time period, although not all would field them.

Soviet industry efforts eventually led to the 31-ton T-28 medium tank fielded in 1934 and the 50-ton T-35 heavy tank fielded in 1935, both of which shared design features and components such as their turrets. The T-28 had a crew of six and the T-35 a crew of eleven. Initially, the maximum armour thickness on the front of the T-35 came to 35mm. That eventually went up to 70mm.

Armament Configuration

The T-35 featured a single elevated 360-degree traversable turret armed with a 76.2mm artillery howitzer. There were four smaller sub-turrets arrayed around and below the elevated main turret. Two had a 45mm anti-tank gun and the other two only a single 7.62mm machine gun.

Instead of mounting a coaxial 7.62mm machine gun with the T-35's 76.2mm main gun, a 7.62mm machine gun appeared in a ball mount on the right-hand front side of the turret. The last few production examples of the T-35 also featured a second 7.62mm machine gun in a ball mount fitted at the rear of the tank's turret. A total of sixty-one examples of the T-35 came off the factory floor between 1931 and 1939.

The two 45mm anti-tank gun-armed sub-turrets of the T-35, one at the front of the vehicle's superstructure and the other at the rear, were each crewed by two men. Each sub-turret also featured a coaxial 7.62mm machine gun. These modified 45mm gun-armed sub-turrets on the T-35 came from the Soviet BT-5 light tank. The two single-man-machine gun-armed turrets on the T-35 came from the T-28 medium tank.

In Service

The Red Army did not employ its T-35 series tanks during the First Russo-Finnish War. It was often seen in Moscow's Red Square pre-war parades, where its size and armament array undoubtedly impressed the assembled visitors.

The Red Army inventory of the T-35 series would see combat in the early months of 1941 during the German invasion. Most, however, were lost to mechanical issues or lack of fuel. A few lasted long enough to see use during the defence of Moscow in the winter of 1941.

Looking for a New Heavy Tank

The search for a replacement for the T-35 began in 1938 and involved two tank design bureaus, one headed by Zh. Ya. Kotin and the other by N. Barykov. The original Red Army requirement for a new heavy tank mandated five turrets, soon reduced to a three-turret configuration.

A more realistic appraisal of the weight and size penalty imposed by having three turrets eventually led to a two-turret requirement. At the same time, the Kirov factory design bureau received permission to submit prototypes of a two-turret and single-turret heavy tank for testing against a two-turreted heavy tank submitted by the Barykov factory design bureau.

The Kotin-designed twin-turreted prototype weighed 61 tons and was labelled the 'SMK', the acronym referring to Sergei Mironovich Kirov, an early and prominent Bolshevik leader assassinated in 1934. The Barykov design bureau's two-turreted submission weighed 65 tons and bore the designation T-100. Both prototypes received power from gasoline engines.

The Kotin team designated its single-turret 76.2mm main gun-armed proto-type the 'KV' in honour of Marshal of the Soviet Union Kliment Voroshilov.

He was the Soviet Defence Minister and Kotin's father-in-law; a case of nepotism at its best.

Descriptions

The original requirement set by the Red Army for the two-turret heavy tank prototypes called for the uppermost turret to feature a 76.2mm main gun. In addition, the top turret was to have a coaxial 7.62mm machine gun and feature 360 degrees of rotation.

The second smaller turret in front of and below the upper turret came with a 45mm gun and a coaxial 7.62mm machine gun. The traverse on the lower turret was restricted by the raised superstructure behind it that mounted the upper turret.

The maximum armour thickness on the turret front of the SMK came to 60mm and 70mm on the turret front of the T-100. The single-turret KV had a much more robust armour protection arrangement. The weight savings from eliminating the second turret and shortening the hull went into thickening the tank's armour.

And The Winner Is?

When the three heavy tank prototypes went through a series of trials in 1939, the KV proved superior to the other submissions. All three prototypes then went off to take part in the First Russo-Finish War to verify the results. Again, the KV proved to be the best choice.

A positive feature of the KV was that its thick armour made it immune to most fielded direct-fire anti-tank weapons. That positive impression led to it receiving authorization for production on 19 December 1939.

Approximately 700 examples of the KV would drive out of the factory doors before the German invasion. Of that number, around 500 were in Red Army service when the attack began. The designation KV-1 did not appear until June 1941. Before that time, the Red Army referred to it as the 'KV with the small turret' or the 'heavy tank KV'.

Total production of the KV-1 series, which ended in 1942, amounted to approximately 3,000 vehicles. There was also a flame-thrower variant of the KV-1 series built in small numbers and designated the KV-8. Due to the space constraints of the KV-1 turret, the KV-8 came with a 45mm main gun in place of the standard 76.2mm main gun to allow room for the flame gun.

KV-1 Description

The five-man KV-1 rode on a torsion bar suspension system that lacked shock absorbers. Depending on the sub-variant, they ranged in weight from 47 to 53 tons. The KV-1 had a 600hp supercharged version of the 500hp diesel engine mounted in the T-34. Maximum road speed topped out at around 20mph, with off-road speed dropping down to 10mph or less.

Like the diesel engine in the T-34, the KV-1 version of the same engine had serious teething problems early on. At one point, a shortage of diesel engines led to about 100 KV-1 tanks leaving the factory with gasoline-powered engines.

The KV-1's five-speed transmission proved to be as unreliable as the four-speed transmission in the early-production T-34. The KV-1's transmission problem lay in the fact that its design came from an American commercial caterpillar tractor design dating from the 1920s, a fact uncovered during a US Army evaluation of a KV-1 supplied by the Soviet Union in 1942.

The old-fashioned transmission combined with an understrength clutch and brake steering system caused endless breakdowns of the KV-1. The tank therefore soon acquired a reputation as mechanically unreliable. The original plans had called for a new transmission design better suited to a heavy tank. However, due to the rush to field the KV-1, the designers had to forgo that idea.

Crew Positions

The KV-1's battlefield effectiveness proved to be limited due to a poorly-designed crew layout. The vehicle commander, located on the right-hand side of the main gun breech, was also made the loader (doctrinally consistent with early T-34s), nor was he provided with an overhead hatch that permitted him to monitor the tactical situation around his vehicle, only a rotating periscope in the turret roof.

Like the T-34, the KV-1 had no turret basket. Except for ten main gun rounds in the turret, the KV-1's rounds were on the hull floor in a two-level arrangement within non-armoured metal containers covered by a rubberized mat.

On the opposite side of the main gun breech sat the gunner, provided with a rotating periscope sight and an articulated telescopic sight. The KV-1 turret could be traversed by the gunner manually or with an electrically-powered motor. As with the T-34, the powered traverse mechanism on the KV-1 tended to be employed for general turret movement with manual adjustment for final target acquisition.

The third crewman assigned to the KV-1 turret was the assistant driver/mechanic. He manned a ball-mounted 7.62mm machine gun located at the rear of the turret bustle in combat. He could open the single roof-mounted turret hatch to operate a 7.62mm machine gun in an anti-aircraft mount.

The driver's position on the KV-1 was located in the centre front hull with the radioman/bow gunner to his left. Unlike the majority of early-production T-34s which lacked radios, most KV-1s had them.

Both the KV-1 driver and radioman/bow gunner shared an overhead hatch in the front hull. There was also an escape hatch under the tank's front hull. Unlike the T-34, which had an interphone system for only the vehicle commander/gunner and driver, on the KV-1 all five crew members had access to an interphone system.

KV-1 Protection

In the spring of 1941, an unfounded belief by a high-ranking Red Army officer that the Germans had been up-gunning their medium tanks led to the up-armouring of the early-production KV-1s by welding on additional RHA armour plates. The add-on RHA plates were bolted to their hulls and turrets.

Unfortunately the up-armouring of the KV-1 and the resulting weight gain proved more than the tank's chassis and powertrain could support, further decreasing the vehicle's already inadequate reliability and leading to the early termination of the up-armouring programme.

Early-production KV-1s had RHA turrets and hulls. Soviet industry eventually designed a CHA turret for the KV-1 series. A British examination of a KV-1 with a CHA turret supplied by the Soviet government stated that its front, sides and rear came in at approximately 100mm. The same report also said that 'The casting of the turret appears to be sound, suggesting good steel foundry practices.' A later-production CHA turret design featured a maximum armour thickness of between 110mm and 120mm.

The same British report went on to say:

A robust cast external mantlet [gun shield] is fitted, but no special precautions appear to have been taken against bullet splash. An unusual feature is the employment of large rubber blocks between the mantlet and the cradle. These are quoted by Russian sources as being fitted for the purpose of reducing impact shocks on the mantlet assembly.

The KV-1 RHA front hull consisted of a stepped arrangement, with the British finding that the front vertical plate was 75mm thick sloped at 32 degrees with a 31mm thick armour plate welded onto it. The glacis plate below and in front of it had a slope of 72 degrees and a thickness of 75mm. The bottom nose plate came to 70mm thick with a slope of 25 degrees, with a 26mm-thick armour plate welded on. The horizontal bottom hull plate was 40mm thick at the front and 32mm on the remainder.

Early Service Use

Like the T-34, the KV-1 proved mostly immune to existing German Army tanks and anti-tank guns in 1941, except when those weapons were using the rare armour-piercing composite rigid (APCR) rounds at short ranges. Pressed into anti-tank service, German 88mm anti-aircraft guns had little trouble in penetrating the KV-1's armour, while German light artillery howitzers firing high explosive could destroy the tank's tracks and suspension.

In a publication titled *Russian Combat Methods in World War II* is the following passage on an encounter between the German Army (reported by senior German officers) and the Red Army that took place in August 1941:

Suddenly enemy tanks of previously unknown type appeared. The tanks overran the armored infantry regiment and broke through into the artillery position. The projectiles of all defense weapons (except the 88mm flak) bounced off the thick enemy armor. The 100 tanks were unable to check the 20 enemy dreadnoughts and suffered losses. Several Czech-built tanks … which had bogged down in the grain fields because of mechanical trouble were flattened by the enemy monsters. The same fate befell a [German] 150mm medium howitzer battery, which kept on firing until the last minute.

Despite the fact that it scored numerous direct hits from as close a range as 200 yards, its heavy shells were unable to put even a single tank out of action. The situation became critical. Only the 88mm flak finally knocked out a few of the Russian KV ls and forced the others to withdraw into the woods.

A senior Red Army officer wrote in his postwar memoirs regarding the KV heavy tanks' first encounter with the German Army: 'The KV tanks literally stunned the enemy. They withstood the fire of every type of gun that the German tanks were armed with. But what a sight they were returning from combat. Their armour was pocked-marked all over, and sometimes even their barrels were pierced.'

Besides some minor tactical success against their foe, KV-1 tanks found themselves hampered by the same issues that dogged the T-34. Untrained crews and poor leadership coupled with overwhelmed logistics resulted in many combat and non-combat losses. Disabled immobile tanks were quickly lost to the rapidly advancing German forces.

The Red Army lost most of its prewar-built KV-1 tanks with little to show by the end of the summer of 1941, with more lost to mechanical-related failures than to combat. A Red Army report from 8 July 1941 noted the following:

In combat, the KV tank demonstrated exceptionally high qualities ... The enemy's medium tank artillery [main guns] can't penetrate its armour. The large losses of the KV tank are explained by the poor technical training of the crew, their insufficient knowledge of the tank's equipment, and the lack of spare parts.

Another Problem Among Many
Unfortunately, before the German invasion the Red Army failed to organize an adequate repair and support service infrastructure. The reason was its focus on having as many tanks built as possible rather than having spare parts. As a result, the Red Army's repair and support services were not up to the task of recovering the KV-1.

Making matters worse, the Red Army had ordered the KV-1 heavy tank without a corresponding order for recovery vehicles large enough and powerful enough to tow disabled vehicles off the field to rear-area repair sites. An example of this issue appears in a Red Army report by an officer listing the problems he observed between June and July 1941:

Repair and evacuation means for the KV tank were lacking. The available Voroshilovets tractors [based on the failed T-24 medium tank chassis] were unable to ensure evacuation; the tractors for towing the KV tanks broke down from the excessive overload. Very frequently, the towing of a tank with another tank took place, and after 10 to 15 kilometres [6 to 9 miles], the towing tank would also break down. The KV tanks can be towed by the Voroshilovets tractors only along roads. On ploughed soil, peat deposits or boggy terrain, a KV tank can only be towed by two tractors.

KV-1 Changes

Early-production KV-1s appeared with the same 76.2mm L-11 main gun found on early-production T-34s. Noticeable external features of the very early-production KV-1s included the lack of a bow machine gun and a large bulbous main gun shield (mantlet). Some early-production KV-1s would see action during the First Russo-Finnish War and the early stages of the German invasion.

Later-production examples of the KV-1 featured a new turret design and gun shield, similar to that on the T-34 series. They also came with the longer-barrelled 76.2mm F-32 main gun and a bow-mounted 7.62mm machine gun operated by the tank's radioman.

KV-1S

Following the KV-1 Model 1942 off the production line was another version designated the KV-1S. The suffix letter 'S' in the designation stood for 'speedy'. As there was no more powerful tank engine to fit into the KV-1S, the primary recourse to improve the vehicle's mobility was to reduce the tank's weight.

Its designers came up with a new smaller, thinner-armoured CHA turret to reduce weight. The hull armour was also thinned compared to that of the later-production KV-1s. New lighter road wheels were mounted. By their efforts, the designers managed to reduce the weight of the KV-1S by slightly more than 5.5 tons. The maximum speed on level roads of the KV-1S was 27mph; much better than the 20mph top speed of the KV-2.

A new transmission and some powertrain improvements also enhanced the KV-1S' reliability and durability compared to its predecessors. As a result of production bottlenecks, some of the early-production KV-1S tanks used the original troublesome transmission. To identify them, they received the designation KV-1SM.

The poor turret crew arrangement of the KV-1 series, with the vehicle commander doubling as the loader, had badly hindered its battlefield effectiveness. With the KV-1S, the designers made the former assistant driver/mechanic the loader, freeing the vehicle commander from that job. To improve the vehicle commander's situational awareness around his tank, he was provided with a cupola, alas without a top hatch.

Testing of KV-1S pre-production pilot vehicles went well, and production tanks began entering Red Army service in August 1942. A total of 780 examples rolled down the assembly lines by the end of 1942. The KV-1S turret retained the 76.2mm main gun of the KV 1 Model 1942. Some experiments took place to see if an 85mm gun could fit into the KV-1S turret, but it proved to be too large.

The retention of the 76.2mm main gun on the KV-1S proved unpopular with a top Red Army general named M. E. Katukov. He informed Stalin in September 1942 that the German Army would soon field a new generation of tanks that would be immune to the 76.2mm gun. As soon as his prediction proved correct, KV-1S production began tailing off, with only 452 examples built in 1943 before production ended. The final count of the KV-1S was a total of 1,232 built.

KV-1 Summary

In a September 1942 meeting with Stalin, a Red Army general stated that Soviet tankers felt that the T-34 was far superior to the KV-1. The latter's higher weight significantly restricted its mobility off-road, which meant it could not keep up with T-34s. Worse, its weight damaged bridges.

If the KV-1 had had a more powerful main gun its design shortcomings might have been forgiven, but efforts to do so proved fruitless. In October 1941, the Red Army decided not to mix medium and heavy tanks in the same units. After that the KV-1 mostly went into homogenous units.

KV-2

Combat experience gained during the First Russo-Finnish War had shown that existing Red Army tanks lacked the firepower necessary to destroy reinforced concrete Finnish Army bunkers. At the prodding of a senior officer commanding troops in Finland, a new heavy breakthrough tank design programme began.

The configuration eventually selected consisted of a newly-designed turret armed with an M-10 152mm howitzer mounted on a KV-1 chassis. A prototype of this stopgap vehicle proved ready for testing in January 1940. Initially it went by the name 'large turret KV', but the designation KV-2 soon appeared.

The initial prototype and a handful of pre-production pilot example KV-2s appeared in January 1940. They featured a relatively complex angled turret design. In February 1940, the Red Army dispatched two to Finland where they performed satisfactorily in their intended role, resulting in approval for full-scale production in November 1940.

The follow-on production version had a more straightforward and simpler to build turret design. It first rolled off the assembly lines in November 1940, continuing until October 1941 with 334 examples completed. Frontal turret armour on the production KV-2s came to 110mm and the turret sides to 75mm. Where the KV-1 had a crew of five, the KV-2 went with a crew of six.

The series production KV-2 appeared with a large and thickly-armoured turret, increasing the vehicle's weight to 57 tons. The added weight badly compromised the chassis of the KV-1 and resulted in even more reliability and mobility issues. Another issue was that the large heavy turret proved un-balanced, making it difficult for the crew to traverse on anything other than level surfaces.

There were some KV-2s stationed in the western military districts of the Soviet Union when the German invasion began. On those occasions when the KV-2s encountered advancing enemy formations, its thick armour provided it with immunity to almost every weapon in the German arsenal except for the 88mm anti-aircraft gun. German soldiers nicknamed the KV-2 the 'Russian Colossus'. A German Army report dated 23 June 1941 stated: 'A KV-2 was hit more than 70 times and not a single round penetrated.'

Fortunately for the German Army, KV-2s were relatively few and far between in the summer of 1941, with most lost to mechanical failure or other non-combat-related causes. A small number of KV-2s would survive long enough to see service during the fighting for Stalingrad, which lasted from August 1942 to February 1943.

KV-3

Kotin, the designer of the original KV-1, had no illusions about the various shortcomings of the vehicle that the Red Army had hurriedly accepted into service. Therefore he had given some thought to designing a new heavy tank for the Red Army's consideration based on lessons learned from the KV-1.

Kotin's proposed new heavy tank eventually received the designation KV-3. Initially, its envisioned armament was a 107mm gun. Later, a 76.2mm main gun became the weapon of choice since it could, in theory, penetrate the armour on German medium tanks of the 1940 time frame.

By early 1941 plans for the KV-3 had progressed far enough so that it was intended for the new heavy tank to replace the KV-1 on the assembly lines beginning in August 1941. As with other tanks still in the developmental stage, the German invasion resulted in the cancellation of the KV-3 with only a single prototype completed. Also cancelled upon the German invasion was all work on two super-heavy tanks designated the KV-4 and KV-5.

KV-13

At the same time that development of the KV-1S was taking place, several design projects were under way to develop a new tank under the umbrella label KV-13. It was intended as a universal tank replacing the T-34 series and the KV-1 series with a maximum weight of 35 tons. Armament would be the same 76.2mm main gun used in the T-34, but the tank had thicker armour than the T-34 series.

The first KV-13 prototype of three eventually built appeared in the spring of 1942. Testing in late summer of 1942 did not go well, with many design shortcomings identified with the powertrain and suspension. Construction of two additional KV-13 prototypes that incorporated lessons learned took place in December 1942. However, by that time the Red Army had already decided that industry would concentrate on building more T-34s and dropped the KV-13 from consideration. The latter's most impressive design feature was its hull, which later served as the chassis for the next Red Army heavy tank.

Slap Something Together

The cancellation of the KV-13 programme left a void in Soviet tank development. However, a team of engineers managed to save the day by coming up with a modified version of the KV-1. They accomplished that goal by taking the hull from the cancelled KV-13 and fitting it with the newly-designed CHA turret of what became the KV-85.

The KV-13's borrowed hull did away with the KV-1's bow machine-gunner's position to save room and improve the front hull contours, improving its ballistic resistance. Stalin approved the tank for production in August 1943. That tank became the IS-85; the prefix 'IS' being the Russian language abbreviation for Iosef Stalin.

Like the KV-1S, the IS-85 had a three-man turret crew, including a vehicle commander, a gunner and a loader. It had a coaxial 7.62mm machine gun and another example in its rear turret bustle. There was also a fixed forward-firing 7.62mm machine gun in the glacis.

The production of the IS-85 began at the end of 1943 and continued until early 1944, with 107 examples completed. None would see combat in its original configuration as growing doubts about the ability of its 85mm main gun to deal with new German tanks led to a decision to fit it with a larger and more potent main gun. Most would eventually be upgraded to a new configuration featuring a 122mm main gun.

Interim Heavy Tank

Because it would take time for the factories and foundries to ramp up for the production of the IS-85, Stalin approved in August 1943 the production of an interim heavy tank that combined the new IS-85 turret mounted on the widened hull of the KV-1S.

The stopgap vehicle became the KV-85, with 130 examples built between September and November 1943. It was the last version of the KV-1 series produced. The frontal turret armour on the KV-85 came to 160mm. As with the IS-85, the designers did away with the bow machine-gunner's position.

A Bigger Gun

The weapon approved for up-gunning the IS-85 was a modified 122mm artillery piece designated the A-19. It was selected as there was an ample supply of the gun and ammunition available and the weapon had performed well in the anti-tank role. The best part was that it proved possible to shoehorn the enormous weapon into the IS-85's existing gun mount.

When mounted in the IS-85 turret, the modified A-19 gun became the D-25T. It had a large double-baffle muzzle brake, the first for a Red Army tank. Testing of the up-gunned IS-85 in November 1943 went well, leading to the decision to place the vehicle into production. The tank initially received the designation IS-122, soon changed to IS-2. In turn, the IS-85 became the IS-1.

As with the KV-1 series, IS-2 had a coaxial 7.62mm machine gun and another in the rear turret bustle. It also had an electrically-powered fixed forward-firing 7.62mm machine gun in the glacis operated by the driver.

A new addition to Red Army tanks of the Second World War was the mounting of a 12.7mm machine gun on the vehicle commander's cupola for use against aerial and ground targets. Frontal turret armour on the IS-2 was 160mm.

The first 150 production examples of the four-man IS-2 model rolled off the factory floor in February 1944. These went into front-line service with special elite units held in reserve until there began a large offensive operation against the enemy, in which they would form the armoured spearhead of the initial assault wave.

Weight was an essential concern with the 51-ton IS-2 design. The Red Army stressed that it could not weigh more than the KV-1 series. Soviet tank designer Alexander A. Morozov would state that 'all basic design decisions for the JS-2 tank were subordinated to the fulfilment of this requirement.' (In the Russian language the letter 'J' appears as an 'I', hence we have the English spelling JS-2 and the Russian spelling IS-2.)

Morozov proved highly critical of late-war German tank designs due to their poor power-to-weight ratio as their designers allowed weights to get out of hand. He noted that compared to German Tiger tanks and the Ferdinand tank destroyer, the IS-2 had thicker frontal armour and still weighed less than its German counterparts.

Armament Issues

Despite the large size of the 122m gun mounted in the IS-2, its armour penetration was not much more than the 75mm main gun on the Panther tank series. When firing at non-armoured targets (the most common engagement), the HE round of the approximately 51-ton IS-2 was very effective due to its size.

The biggest fault with the IS-2's 122mm gun proved to be the size of ammunition. It was too heavy for a single loader; therefore it was made as a two-piece round, with the projectile going into the weapon's breech first, followed by the cartridge case containing the propellant. This slowed down loading, which reduced its maximum rate of fire.

Combined with the turret's tight confines, the IS-2 could carry only twenty-eight main gun rounds. In comparison, the KV-1S carried 114 rounds of 76.2mm main gun ammunition and the IS-1 had stowage for 59 of its 85mm main gun rounds.

Improving the IS-2

The first examples of the IS-2 initially entered into combat in April 1944 and proved to be well-liked. So popular were they that the Red Army had industry increase the production rate of the tank. Eventually an improved version with the same main gun but with a new redesigned glacis appeared. It provided superior ballistic protection due to its more sloping design than the stepped glacis of early-production examples inherited from the KV-1.

Other improvements to later-production IS-2s included replacing the manually-operated screw-type breechblock with a semi-automatic breechblock that speeded up the tank's rate of fire from one to two rounds per minute. In addition, there was also a new wider gun shield. By the time production ended in 1945, a total of 3,854 examples of the IS-2 series had come out of the factory doors.

The Next Big Step

Even while Soviet industry's production of the IS-2 was under way, it began work on a next-generation heavy tank at the behest of the Red Army to feature the IS-2's 122mm main gun. The Red Army's design benchmarks for an IS-2 replacement included the ability to resist the fire of the AP rounds fired by the 88mm main gun of the German Tiger II.

To optimize the ability of an IS-2 replacement to resist penetration by high-velocity anti-tank projectiles, its designers developed a large, thickly-armoured and highly-sloped hemispherical turret. It was a far cry from the more slab-sided turrets of the IS-2. Maximum armour thickness on the newly-designed turret came to 230mm. The two thick, sharply-angled armour plates welded together for the glacis had a maximum armour thickness of 120mm.

A prototype of the new heavy tank was shown to senior Red Army armour commanders in December 1944, meeting with their approval and eventually becoming the IS-3. Ten pre-production pilot vehicles received authorization for construction, with testing to begin in the following month.

Successfully passing all tests, the four-man IS-3 received authorization for production. The first examples rolled out of the factory doors in May 1945, too late to see combat in the collapse of Nazi Germany.

Like the IS-2, the approximate 55-ton IS-3 had a coaxial 7.62mm machine gun. However, it lacked the rear turret bustle 7.62mm machine gun of previous heavy tanks. As with the IS-2 series, the IS-3 came with a turret roof-mounted 12.7mm machine gun. Its maximum speed on level roads was the same as that of the IS-2, about 23mph.

The IS-3 debuted at a victory parade held in Berlin, Germany on 7 September 1945, when fifty-two of them rolled past the assembled visitors, much to the astonishment of the Western Allied military leaders. They were not aware of the vehicle's existence before that point in time.

Despite its positive impression made at the time, the IS-3, in reality, was far from the perfect tank. Like the IS-2, it only had authorized stowage for twenty-eight main gun rounds. Due to the haste in fielding the tank, it remained besieged by a host of unresolved design shortcomings that were never resolved, even in the postwar era.

(**Opposite, above**) Following the First World War, the British government supplied about seventy of its Mark V heavy tanks, pictured here, to anti-Bolshevik forces. The tanks eventually fell into Red Army hands. The eight-man tank weighed about 32 tons and, depending on the model, was armed with two 6-pounder (57mm) guns and four machine guns, or six machine guns and no 6-pounders. Four of them would last long enough in Red Army service to see combat during the opening stage of the German invasion of June 1941. (*Dreamstime*)

(**Below**) During its time in Great Britain in the 1920s, while looking to buy tanks for technical evaluation, the Red Army's purchasing committee happened to observe the prototype multi-turreted Vickers A1W1 Independent heavy tank pictured here. Four of the vehicle's five turrets had machine guns; the largest turret had a 6-pounder (57mm) main gun. When informed that neither the eight-man vehicle nor its technical data was for sale, the Red Army acquired the plans for the 36-ton vehicle by deceit. (*Dreamstime*)

ДА ЗДРАВСТВУЕТ
ВСЕСОЮЗНАЯ
КОММУНИСТИЧЕСКАЯ
ПАРТИЯ
БОЛЬШЕВИКОВ-
ПЕРЕДОВОЙ ОТРЯД
ТРУДЯЩИХСЯ
СОВЕТСКОГО
СОЮЗА!

(**Opposite, above**) The Red Army ordered Soviet industry to build an up-gunned version of the multi-turreted Vickers A1W1 Independent heavy tank. An example of the tank, designated the T-35, is pictured here. Like the British tank, the T-35 had five turrets. The largest was armed with a 76.2mm howitzer and a 7.62mm machine gun. Two of the other four turrets each had 45mm guns and a coaxial 7.62mm machine gun. The other two turrets featured only a single 7.62mm machine gun. (*Dreamstime*)

(**Opposite, below**) German soldiers stand around a Red Army T-35 heavy tank. Most saw little combat in the summer of 1941 due to reasons such as mechanical breakdown or running out of fuel. T-35 production took place between 1933 and 1938, with a total of sixty-one examples built. Only the larger elevated turret had 360 degrees of rotation; the smaller turrets had necessarily limited traverse due to the design. (*Author's collection*)

(**Above**) As seen here in a prewar parade, the last six production examples of the T-35 appeared with sloping armoured turrets. Armour thickness on the turret front was 70mm compared to the 30mm on the fifty-five earlier-production examples. Up-armouring the tanks led to an increase in weight from around 50 to 60 tons. Despite the weight increase, the vehicle retained its original 500hp gasoline-powered engine. (*Author's collection*)

Development of a suitable replacement for the less than successful T-35 heavy tank led the Red Army to task two different design bureaus with creating something better. The original Red Army requirement called for a five-turreted vehicle, which was eventually reduced to a two-turreted vehicle. Pictured here is an artist's impression of the approximately 65-ton heavy tank design prototype put forward by the design bureau headed by N. Barykov labelled the 'T-100'. (*Dreamstime*)

The second design bureau tasked with designing and developing a new heavy tank was headed by Zhozef Kotin. He too came up with a twin-turreted heavy tank design as specified. Kotin, however, had the foresight to realize that twin-turreted tanks were already obsolete. He therefore proposed the design of a new single-turreted heavy tank eventually embraced by the Red Army as the KV. Pictured here is an early-production example armed with the L-11 76.2mm main gun. (*Author's collection*)

Pictured here is a later-production example of the KV armed with the F-32 76.2mm main gun. Like early-production examples armed with the L-11 76.2mm main gun, the vehicle here has a rolled homogenous armour (RHA) turret and lacks a bow 7.62mm machine gun. The KV's original designation in Red Army shipping documents was 'KV with Small Turret' or 'KV L-11'. In March 1941 the designation 'KV-1' was issued. *(Dreamstime)*

An early production KV-1 has been caught in the woods and hit, evident from the smoke coming out of the vehicle. The tank carried an authorized allotment of 111 76.2mm main gun rounds stored between the turret and hull, with most stored in the hull. *(Patton Museum)*

(**Above**) The KV-1 pictured here received power from a 600hp diesel engine, an uprated version of the T-34's 500hp diesel engine. Early KV-1 engines seldom lasted more than 100 running hours. The tank's clutch also proved unequal to the demands placed upon it and often failed. A British wartime report noted with surprise that Soviet industry used a clutch brake steering system on a tank as heavy as the KV-1. Adding to the tank's poor mechanical reliability was an obsolete transmission design. (*Author's collection*)

(**Opposite, above**) The F-32 76.2mm main gun on new-production KV-1s was eventually replaced by a longer-barrelled version designated the ZiS-5, seen here. By 1942 most new-production KV-1s came out of factories with the ZiS-5, although when temporary shortages of the gun occurred, the F-34 76.2mm main gun of the T-34 took its place. The same gun shield was used for KV-1s armed with the F-32, ZiS-5 or the F-34. (*Dreamstime*)

(**Below**) Despite their superior level of armour protection and firepower, performance of the 500 or so KV-1s facing the German armies in 1941 proved extremely disappointing. A couple of factors contributed to this included poorly-trained crews combined with shortages of everything including fuel and ammunition. Pictured here is a knocked-out KV-1 tank armed with an F-32 76.2mm main gun. (*Author's collection*)

As with the T-34, Soviet industry eventually switched to making cast homogeneous armour (CHA) turrets on KV-1s, as appears on the tank pictured here. Combat experience would lead to a series of armour upgrades for the CHA turret and rolled homogenous armour (RHA) for the hull beginning in 1942. The KV-1's poor automotive performance compared to that of the T-34 meant that it could not keep up with the latter in offensive operations, eventually leading to units being equipped with only KV-1s. (*Author's collection*)

Despite its label of a heavy tank, the KV-1 was a much more compact design than that of the American first-generation M4 series medium tank, as is apparent from this photograph. Both tanks had five-man crews with a turret crew of three. The KV-1 had a length of 22.6ft, a width of almost 12ft and a height of 9.7ft. It weighed about 16 tons more than the M4 pictured and was much more heavily-armoured. (*Author's collection*)

A factory overhauling KV-1s with both RHA and CHA turreted models is pictured here. Improved German tank and anti-tank guns forced the thickening of armour on later-production KV-1s. That thickening is seen in the flared-out bottom of the CHA turret in the foreground. Continued up-armouring without parallel improvements to its power-plant led to the KV-1 becoming ever more unreliable. (*Author's collection*)

(**Above**) From the turret bustle of a KV-1 tank looking forward. The gunner's position is on the left-hand side of the main gun and the vehicle commander/loader's position is on the right-hand side. The third crewman in the KV-1 turret, labelled the assistant driver/mechanic, manned the 7.62mm machine gun located in the rear turret bustle. Having the vehicle commander/loader switch positions with the assistant driver/mechanic was not feasible as the latter's position had no overhead vision devices. (*Author's collection*)

(**Opposite, above**) Looking rearward in the turret of a KV-1 is the assistant driver/mechanic's position with his rear turret bustle 7.62mm machine gun. His two overhead periscopes are both visible in this image. Note the storage arrangement for the machine gun's sixty-one-round pan magazines. Also visible are two of the five-round storage racks on either side of the turret bustle machine gun for main gun rounds. Early KVs had authorized storage for 116 76.2mm main gun rounds, which eventually dropped to 98 on late-production examples. (*Author's collection*)

(**Opposite, below**) A view from the rear of a KV-1's lower hull fighting compartment from just in front of the engine compartment firewall. In the foreground is the metal conduit containing the electrical cable to the turret traverse motor. On either side of the lower hull are storage racks for pan magazines for the vehicle's 7.62mm machine guns. In the centre background is the driver's seat backrest and forward-facing periscope. (*Author's collection*)

(**Opposite, above**) A flame-thrower version of the KV-1 appeared and received the designation of the KV-8. Due to the size of the flame-gun and associated plumbing to the weapon's fuel tanks in the fighting compartment, it proved impossible to retain the standard 76.2mm main gun. The replacement was a smaller 45mm gun allowing the tank to defend itself when the flame-gun's fuel supply had been exhausted. (*Author's collection*)

(**Opposite, below**) Combat experience during the First Russo-Finnish War demonstrated that existing Red Army tank guns could not destroy stoutly-built Finnish Army bunkers. The quick fix involved a new turret design mounting the 152mm Howitzer M1938 (with the factory designation of the M-10). That vehicle became the 'KV with Large Turret' or 'KV M-10' in Red Army shipping documents. Later designated as the 'KV-2', the vehicle pictured here is a very early-production example. (*Dreamstime*)

(**Above**) Compared to the 50-ton KV-1, the massive turret of the six-man KV-2 brought the vehicle's weight up to around 57 tons, badly overloading the existing KV-1 chassis which was already plagued by design issues. The KV-2's additional weight, as can be imagined, also affected the vehicle's off-road mobility. Due to the KV-2's top-heavy turret, it didn't prove easy to travel anywhere other than on level ground. (*Dreamstime*)

An artist's illustration of a KV-2 that has taken numerous hits on its turret. As with the KV-1s, German gunners found their standard 37mm towed anti-tank guns useless against the KV-2. The Red Army's heavy tanks would create havoc among some German infantry and light tank-equipped units. If available, the German towed 88mm anti-aircraft gun proved capable of destroying both the KV-1 and KV-2. (*Dreamstime*)

By late 1941 it was apparent to all, from top Red Army leadership down to the tankers themselves, that the KV-1 was a failure. The general heading the Red Army's armoured forces pressed for a single tank design that could fulfil all the roles of the existing Soviet light, medium and heavy tanks. In response Zhozef Kotin, who designed the KV-1 and was well aware of the tank's shortcomings, came up with a new lighter version that became the KV-1S pictured here. (*Dreamstime*)

The weight-saving measures Kotin employed for the KV1-S included thinning armour on both the vehicle's hull and turret. The latter, a new design, was smaller in dimensions than the KV 1's original CHA turret. Less volume meant less armour required and, in turn, less weight. Kotin also upgraded the tank's powertrain to close the gap between the T-34 and KV1-S operational parameters. Unfortunately the KV1-S retained the KV-1's 76.2mm main gun, which was in all respects no better than that of the cheaper, faster and more-reliable T-34. (*Dreamstime*)

(**Above**) The turret crew arrangement on the KV-1S with an example pictured here was an improvement over that on the KV-1. The former assistant driver/mechanic in the KV-1 turret became the loader, freeing the vehicle commander from that responsibility. He could now concentrate on what was going on outside the confines of his tank. This rearrangement of functions led to fitting a commander's cupola on the roof to improve visibility, although it is not seen on this particular vehicle. There was no overhead hatch in the cupola. (*Dreamstime*)

(**Opposite, above**) Efforts to fit an 85mm main gun and three-man turret crew into the KV-1S turret failed. Kotin's design team therefore designed a new larger three-man turret that provided room for an 85mm gun and turret crew for mounting on the future IS-1 heavy tank, an improved KV-1 series tank with a new name. Due to delays with IS-1 production, the new 85mm gun-armed turret went onto the chassis of 136 examples of a slightly modified KV-1S, creating the KV-85 pictured here. (*Author's collection*)

Like the KV-1S, the KV-85 had a cupola for the vehicle commander and, like that on its predecessor, it lacked an overhead hatch. The 85mm main gun that went into the turret of the KV-85 was the same D-5T gun that armed early-production T-34-85s, hence the similarity of the former's gun shield to that of early-production T-34-85s. Very early-production examples of the KV-85 had a 7.62mm bow machine gun, later done away with, bringing the crew number down to four men. (*Author's collection*)

(**Above**) The replacement for both the KV-1S and the KV-85 was the four-man IS-2 heavy tank pictured here, armed with a 122mm main gun. It featured both a redesigned turret and hull with a host of powertrain improvements. It had a large double-baffle muzzle brake. The IS-2 weighed about 45 tons. By comparison, the German Panther medium tank weighed about 50 tons. (*Pierre-Olivier Buan*)

(**Opposite, above**) The IS-2 pictured here is a wartime production example as it lacks the small upper hull side storage compartments that appeared on postwar modernized vehicles. The tank was approximately 32ft long, had a width of about 10ft and was around 9ft tall. The German Panther tank had a height of 10ft. Because of the size and weight of the 122mm rounds fired by the IS-2, it used separately-loaded ammunition, restricting the rate of fire to only two or three rounds per minute. (*Pierre-Olivier Buan*)

(**Opposite, below**) The IS-2 in the foreground of this wartime image is a late-production example with a wider new gun shield design and a sloping glacis, in contrast to the stepped glacis of earlier-production examples. Another improvement to late-production IS-2s was replacing the manually-operated interrupted screw breechblock with a semi-automatic breechblock that increased the gun's rate of fire. (*Author's collection*)

(**Above**) Even as production of the IS-2 continued, Soviet industry had already begun designing a new version of the vehicle with increased frontal armour protection, making it immune to the AP rounds fired from the 88cm KwK-43 gun that armed the Tiger B (Tiger II) heavy tank. Soviet designers came up with a large, thickly-armoured and highly-sloped semi-hemispherical turret to achieve that goal. Maximum armour protection on the front of that new turret was 230mm. The thick sharply-angled glacis had a maximum thickness of 120mm. (*Pierre-Olivier Buan*)

(**Opposite, above**) In this photograph we see the driver's compartment of an IS-3. Visible are the instrument panel and steering levers on either side of the driver's seat. On the right-hand side of the photograph is the gear shift lever. As with earlier heavy tanks beginning with the KV-1, the IS-3 received power from a 600hp diesel engine that provided a top speed on level roads of about 23mph. (*Chris Hughes*)

(**Opposite, below**) The four-man IS-3 did not have a vehicle commander's cupola. Instead it had a large overhead two-piece hatch that could be raised as one piece as seen on this postwar IS-3 (identified by the small upper side hull compartments) or separately. The tank is about 35ft long with a width of around 11ft and a height of approximately 9ft, not counting the 12.7mm machine gun customarily fitted on the turret roof. (*Ian Wilcox*)

The derelict IS-3 pictured here has no doubt seen better days during its career. Due to the lack of a turret bustle, the tank's twenty-eight separately-loaded projectiles were stored upright around the inside of the turret ring, the propellant charges being stored in the bottom of the vehicle's fighting compartment. Like previous KV series tanks, the IS-3 rode on a torsion bar suspension system. Due to the layout of the vehicle's glacis, tankers nicknamed it 'the Pike'. (*Dreamstime*)

Chapter Five

Artillery

The Red Army had a massive inventory of artillery pieces in service when the German Army invaded in June 1941. Despite huge wartime losses, by the end of the Second World War it had grown even larger. Artillery in this context included conventional towed artillery pieces, anti-tank guns, anti-aircraft guns and mortars; mortars were the most numerous artillery pieces throughout the war. To the Red Army, artillery was 'the God of War'.

Small-Calibre Anti-Tank Guns

The Red Army's first dedicated anti-tank gun was a licence-built copy of a German-designed 37mm anti-tank gun. This Soviet industry-modified version became the 37mm Anti-Tank Gun M1930 (1-K), with 509 examples completed between 1931 and 1932. The suffix designation is a code identifying the factory that built the weapon.

The 37mm Anti-Tank Gun M1930 (1-K) fired a roughly 2lb armour-piercing (AP) round with a muzzle velocity of 2,500ft/s that could penetrate the frontal armour on most existing tanks of the early 1930s. There was no high-explosive (HE) round for the weapon.

The Red Army then sought an anti-tank gun able to fire a more potent AP and an HE round; Soviet industry scaled up the weapon, creating the 45mm Anti-Tank Gun M1937 (53-K). Approximately 37,354 examples of the 1,234lb weapon came off the assembly lines between 1937 and 1943. It fired a roughly 3lb AP round with a muzzle velocity of 2,493ft/s.

To improve the M1937 (53-K) performance, the Red Army had Soviet industry design a longer-barrelled version with a muzzle velocity of 2,584ft/s, increasing armour penetration. The redesigned weapon became the 45mm Anti-Tank Gun M1942 (M-42), with about 11,000 completed between 1942 and 1945.

In a passage from the book titled *Panzer Killers: Anti-Tank Warfare on the Eastern Front*, a Red Army soldier who served on a 45mm anti-tank gun crew recalls that Soviet infantry nicknamed their M 42 guns as 'Farewell, Motherland' or the 'Crew's Death' because of the crews' high losses in combat.

From a US Army wartime publication titled *Tactical and Technical Trends No. 31* dated 12 August 1943 in the article titled 'Tactics of Russian Anti-Tank Regiments' is the following passage:

In any circumstances, guns will only open fire on tanks from a distance of 500 to 600 yards and will do nothing before that to disclose their position.

In order to attack the gun position, a tank, allowing for a speed of 12 miles per hour, will require two minutes. During this time, allowing for average conditions of fire, 12–14 shots can be fired. Let us suppose that the percentage of effective hits will be 20–25. This means that each gun will put out of action two to three tanks before it is annihilated, assuming that the enemy continues to advance with complete disregard for losses. The whole regiment under such conditions can put out of action several dozen tanks in one attack, and moreover, only the batteries in the first echelon will suffer substantial losses.

A Larger Anti-Tank Gun

In anticipation of the German Army fielding ever more thickly-armoured tanks, in 1940 the Red Army directed Soviet industry to develop a more powerful anti-tank gun. The result was the more than 1-ton 57mm Anti-Tank Gun M1941 (ZiS-2), with the first 371 examples appearing in service before the German invasion.

As the existing 45mm anti-tank guns proved themselves able to deal with German medium tanks during 1941, the Red Army ended M1941 (ZiS-2) production in December 1941.

Sliding Breechblocks

The Red Army's 57mm anti-tank gun and its predecessors all had semi-automatic sliding breechblocks. Upon firing, the guns automatically ejected spent cartridge cases and left the breechblocks in the open position to facilitate the rapid insertion of another round. The motion of a semi-automatic sliding breechblock can be either horizontal or vertical.

A positive design feature of these breechblocks was their manufacturing simplicity. Their downside was the necessity of using a comparatively large breech section capable of withstanding the stresses of firing, adding weight to the gun's rear area.

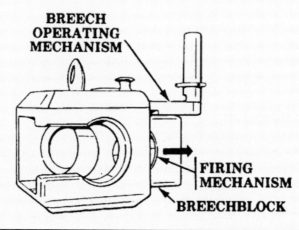

From a publication titled *Russian Combat Methods in World War Two* published in November 1950 is the following passage by a senior German officer:

The anti-tank gun was an auxiliary weapon from which the Russian soldier never separated. Wherever the Russian infantryman was, anti-tank defence could be expected by his enemy. At times it appeared to the Germans that each Russian infantryman had an anti-tank gun or anti-tank rifle, just as infantrymen of other armies had ordinary rifles. The Russian moved his anti-tank defence everywhere with great skill. It was to be found even where no German tank attacks might be expected.

As the German Army fielded better-armoured tanks in 1942 and 1943, the Red Army had Soviet industry restart production of a slightly modified version of the 57mm Anti-Tank Gun M1941 (ZiS-2) in 1943, with the new designation of the M1943 (ZiS-2). Production continued until 1945, resulting in the construction of approximately 10,000 examples. It fired a 7lb AP round with a muzzle velocity of 3,300ft/s.

The Red Army, at the tail end of the Second World War, fielded in small numbers two new large-calibre anti-tank guns. These included the approximately 2-ton 85mm Divisional Gun (D-44) and the roughly 4-ton 100mm Field Gun M1944 (BS-3). Both fired fixed rounds, had semi-automatic sliding breechblocks and were dual-purpose weapons capable of indirect fire when required.

76mm Divisional Guns

When the German Army invaded, one of the Red Army artillery pieces encountered was the 76mm Divisional Gun M1902. It had seen service during the First World War with the Imperial Russian Army. A total of 2,500 examples came off the assembly lines by the time production concluded in 1931.

Modernized by Soviet industry, the M1902 evolved into the M1902/30. It had a pole (single) trail and weighed about 1.5 tons. The gun fired an HE round at a muzzle velocity of 2,172ft/s and came with an interrupted screw breech mechanism.

Eventually an AP round appeared for the M1902/30. All Red Army towed artillery pieces had a secondary role as direct-fire anti-tank weapons. Like the Model 1902, the M1902/30 remained in service long enough to see combat during the early stages of the German Army invasion.

New Anti-Tank Munitions
Soviet industry began manufacturing hyper-velocity armour-piercing (HVAP) rounds and high-explosive anti-tank (HEAT) rounds with shaped-charge warheads in 1942. They were basing their designs on captured German ammunition. The HVAP rounds (referred to as tungsten carbide subcalibre rounds by the Red Army) went to its high-velocity anti-tank guns. The HEAT rounds went to its low-velocity artillery pieces such as howitzers.

A German officer's report documented an early engagement with the Red Army in June 1941:

> Late in the morning, light Russian artillery suddenly joined the battle very effectively with observed fire from battery after battery. Every battery moved speedily into firing position upon arrival and opened fire; as a result, it was possible to estimate approximately the number of batteries firing. It was very difficult, however, to identify the extremely well-concealed observation posts, whereas a few poorly defiladed firing positions were easily located from the muzzle flashes of the weapons. The Russian battery commanders, based on keen observation, combated every German movement and every machine gun they had identified in an exposed firing position by means of a flawless bracketing method passing over into ladder fire. This meticulously accurate artillery fire caused great losses among the German troops and had a damaging morale effect on them.

Interim 76mm Divisional Gun

The Red Army's stopgap replacement for the M1902/1930 bore the designation M1933. It was a progressively improved version of the M1902/30. In its continued standardization policy, the barrel of the M1933 went onto the box trail carriage of the 122mm Howitzer M1910/30 already in production.

The weight of the M1933 was almost 2 tons due to its much longer barrel. It fired an HE round at a muzzle velocity of 2,350ft/s. The maximum range was approximately 8 miles. It had an interrupted screw breech mechanism. Some would remain in service long enough to see combat when the German Army invaded.

Never Stopped Trying

Soviet industry continued to refine the design of the 76mm gun. The designers strived for a new weapon that could function as either a standard artillery piece or an anti-aircraft gun, although it never saw use in the latter role. As a result, the weapon became the 76mm Divisional Gun M1936 (F-22).

Unlike its predecessor's box trail, the almost 2-ton M1936 (F-22) had a modern split-trail carriage. Rather than the unsprung spoked wooden wheels of the earlier 76mm divisional guns, it rode on solid rubber tyres fitted to metal hubs with a suspension system.

The gun had a rate of fire of fifteen rounds per minute and a maximum range of about 8 miles. It had a semi-automatic sliding breechblock and fired a 14lb HE or AP round at a muzzle velocity of 2,316ft/s. While prototypes of the M1936 (F-22) appeared with muzzle brakes, the production examples did not.

Due to the weapon's modern design features, the two factories assigned to build it had problems in meeting their production goals. Making matters worse, those issued had reliability problems in the field. As a result, the M1936 (F-22) construction concluded in 1939, with the number built capped at around 3,000.

Some of those would see service in the Red Army until the end of the Second World War in ever-diminishing numbers.

Enemy Use

As with so many other captured Red Army artillery pieces, the Germans employed the M1936 (F-22) against its former owners. The Germans initially used it as an artillery piece and later as an anti-tank gun sporting a muzzle brake.

The Germans rechambered the M1936 (F-22) to accommodate a larger German-manufactured cartridge case for dealing with enemy tanks. The larger propellant charge increased the weapon's muzzle velocity and armour penetration. The weapon is best known for its use as the armament for the German Marder II and Marder III tank destroyers.

Up Next

The next Red Army iteration of 76mm guns was the 76mm Divisional Gun M1939 (USV), with the suffix letters standing for '76-36'. The number '36' represents the year 1936, in which the design won Red Army approval.

Unlike previous 76mm guns with the recoil and counter-recoil (recuperator) cylinders located underneath the gun's barrel, the M1939 (USV) recoil and counter-recoil cylinders were divided between the top and bottom of the barrel to improve cooling and reduce heat build-up during prolonged firing.

Like the previous dedicated anti-tank guns and earlier-generation 76mm guns, the M1939 (USV) had a semi-automatic sliding breechblock. The gun and carriage of the weapon weighed in at around 1.5 tons. It had a modern recoil system and breech and rode on rubber tyres with steel hubs fitted with a suspension system. The weapon's maximum rate of fire was fifteen rounds per minute, with its range topping out at about 8 miles. It fired a 13lb HE or AP round with a muzzle velocity of 2,218ft/s.

Restarting Production

Before the German Army invasion, the Red Army had production of the M1939 (USV) halted due to the erroneous belief that the armour on new German

---

Counter-Recoil

There are two types of counter-recoil systems: spring-operated and hydro-pneumatic-operated. The Red Army's conventional artillery pieces employed the latter.

The pneumatic cylinder portion of a counter-recoil mechanism is gas-filled (air or nitrogen) under very high pressure and contains a piston rod. The hydro (liquid) portion of the counter-recoil mechanism keeps the gas from leaking from the system.

When the weapon fires and its barrel recoils, the gas in the counter-recoil cylinder compresses even more. This pressure, acting on the piston rod in the cylinder, returns the barrel to its original firing position ('in-battery').

medium tanks was thicker than thought, rendering its 76mm gun inventory semi-useless in the anti-tank role. This led the Red Army to adopt the 107mm Divisional Gun M1940 (M-60) gun in October 1940. Upon the German Army invasion, the Red Army cancelled the gun after only 132 examples had come out of the factory doors.

There were various reasons for ending the 107mm M1940 (M-60) gun production, including insufficient prime movers to tow the heavy weapon. Another problem was its complex design that made it challenging to build quickly and maintain.

In place of the cancelled 107mm M1940 (M60), the Red Army had Soviet industry restart production of the M1939 (USV). As a result, an additional 8,622 examples of the latter came down the assembly lines by 1942. By that time, the Red Army's inventory of 76mm guns primarily saw service as direct-fire anti-tank guns. Their HE rounds were no longer seen as effective on the battlefield due to a lack of explosive punch.

In the January 1943 issue of *Intelligence Bulletin* in an article titled 'Russian Anti-Tank Tactics' the following passage appears:

> Fortifying 45 and 76mm gun positions is hard work, but it pays large dividends in combating German tanks. Crews are taught not only to dig in and to camouflage quickly but also to mine sectors in front of their batteries. When time permits, two or three alternate positions are dug for each gun and are used to confuse the enemy in spotting our gun positions. Artillery fire from these positions is also frequently imitated in order to draw enemy fire.

As was the case with other Red Army artillery pieces captured by the Germans, the M1939 (USV) found itself pressed into service against its former owners. It was used as a dedicated anti-tank gun fitted with a muzzle brake and with a secondary role as a field gun.

Artillery Ammunition

All the Red Army's dedicated anti-tank guns fired one-piece complete rounds, more commonly known as 'fixed rounds'. The propelling charge fits loosely in the cartridge case, which is crimped rigidly to the projectile. The primer resides in the base of the cartridge case.

Those artillery rounds with the provision for adjusting the propelling charge before firing are known as 'semi-fixed rounds'. Unlike fixed rounds where the cartridge case is crimped rigidly to the projectile, the semi-fixed round cartridge cases fit loosely over the projectile. The propelling charge is accessible for adjustment.

When the various components of artillery rounds – the projectile, propelling charge and primer – are loaded into an artillery piece separately, they are known as 'separate-loaded rounds'.

The Final 76mm Gun Iteration

Without a specific request from the Red Army, a Soviet design bureau member decided in 1940 to come up with a new 76mm gun that would answer criticisms levelled at previous models, such as their size and weight.

To do so, he took the barrel from the M1936 (USV), added a muzzle brake and mated it to the carriage of the 57mm Anti-Tank Gun Model 1943 (ZiS-2). The resulting combination impressed all who saw it demonstrated. The weapon became the 76mm Divisional Gun M1942 (ZiS-3).

Between December 1941 and 1945 more than 100,000 examples of the M1942 (ZiS-3) were produced. A modified form armed the SU-76 self-propelled gun.

The M1942 (ZiS-3) weighed 2,460lb and a well-trained crew could fire up to twenty-five rounds per minute for a short time, although a more realistic rate of fire was ten rounds per minute. The maximum range came to around 8 miles in the indirect fire mode. It had a semi-automatic sliding breechblock and fired 14lb AP rounds at a muzzle velocity of 2,231ft/s.

In the more typical direct-fire mode, the M1942 (ZiS-3) proved potent enough to defeat the armour on German Panzer IV medium tanks. The frontal armour on the Panther and Tiger made them almost entirely immune to the M1942 (ZiS-3). However, their side and rear armour proved vulnerable at certain ranges. A senior Red Army officer would note that

It is practically impossible to penetrate the frontal armour of all the new German tanks with the existing 45mm and 76mm guns of the battalion, regimental and divisional anti-tank artillery from a typical range of fire. The

---

Artillery Definitions

The term 'gun' includes all classes of firearms. The word 'cannon' encompasses all artillery pieces. Within the category of cannons, guns typically have long barrels, high muzzle velocities and flat trajectories below 45 degrees. Artillery pieces classified as guns typically see use in long-range, indirect fire.

A 'howitzer' is a comparatively short cannon with a medium muzzle velocity. Howitzers are typically fired at steep elevations so that their rounds can reach targets hidden from flat-trajectory guns. Variations in propelling charges (bag charges) change a round's trajectory and range.

Within a book titled *The Guns: 1939–1945* by weapons expert Ian V. Hogg is a passage going into more detail on howitzers:

For a given calibre, the howitzer will generally fire a heavier shell than a gun. It will have a shorter range and itself weigh rather less; the whole reason being the lesser velocity leads to less stress on the shell in the bore – hence the heavier shell – and less stress on the mounting itself – hence the lighter equipment.

Sometimes the distinction between an artillery gun and a howitzer is blurred due to the development of 'gun-howitzers' that could perform both roles.

heavy Tiger tanks were invulnerable to the guns of the specified calibres. The available 76mm and 45mm APDS [armour-piercing discarding sabot] shells could be effective only against the side armour of the Tiger tank and the frontal armour of the new German Pz-III and Pz-IV medium tanks only from short ranges (not more than 200 metres) [219 yards].

Another Red Army anti-tank gunner recalled how they organized themselves and their M1942 (ZiS-3) guns in preparation for battle:

Two holes were made to the left and right of a gun's wheels – one for the gunner, the other for the loader. Practically, ZiS-3 guns didn't require simultaneous presence of the entire crew near the gun. Moreover, it was usually enough for only one person to be present. The gunner, after firing, could hide himself in his hole while the loader would drive the next shell into the barrel. Now the gunner could take his place, aim and fire and the loader would be taking cover at that time. Even after a direct hit into the gun, at least one of the two had a chance to survive. The other crew members were spread out through the holes, side 'pockets' of the trench.

122mm Howitzers

The Red Army had industry modernize two pre-First World War Russian Imperial Army artillery pieces in the 1930s. The first was derived from a German design and originally bore the label of the 122mm Howitzer M1909. Modernized, it became the 122mm Howitzer M1909/37 with approximately 1,000 examples going through the upgrade process. The weight came in at about 1.5 tons.

The second howitzer was a French design that became the 122mm Howitzer M1910. Modernized, it received the designation 122mm Howitzer M1910/30, with up to 6,000 examples upgraded. It weighed a little over 1.5 tons and, like its predecessor, rode on a box trail carriage with unsprung wooden-spoked wheels.

The M1909/37 had a semi-automatic sliding breechblock; the M1910/30 had an interrupted screw breech mechanism. The rate of fire for the former came to two rounds per minute and the latter five to six rounds per minute. Both howitzers used separately-loaded ammunition and remained in service with the Red Army throughout the Second World War.

The Final Version

The last 122mm howitzer to enter Red Army service before the Second World War proved to be the 122mm Howitzer M1938 (M-30). The almost 3-ton cannon had a rate of fire of five to six rounds per minute. It fired a 48lb HE round with a muzzle velocity of 1,503ft/s; a modified form of the howitzer armed the SU-122 self-propelled gun.

The range of the M1938 (M-30) topped out at around 7 miles. It had an interrupted screw breech mechanism and used separately-loaded ammunition. Approximately 18,000 examples of the M1938 (M-30) came out of the factory doors between 1940 and 1945.

In a passage taken from a translated postwar Soviet Army report found on the Tank Archives blog is the following information on the 122mm Howitzer M1938 (M-30):

> The 122mm mod. 1938 howitzer showed itself well as an infantry support measure when destroying medium fortifications (wire obstacles, trenches, pillboxes with light coverage, dugouts).
>
> The range and rate of fire are entirely satisfactory for completion of tasks assigned to this gun in various battle conditions and types of fire. However, the 122mm howitzer cannot be used specifically as an anti-tank gun as it is heavy, not mobile, and has low muzzle velocity.
>
> The 122mm howitzer has low dispersion due to its weight. It satisfies all requirements and demands given by infantry. As a divisional system, it is sufficiently maneuverable. A wheeled artillery tractor is most appropriate for towing this gun (three-axle, like a Studebaker).

Field Artillery Definitions

Most of the Red Army's artillery pieces fell under the general heading of field artillery. A Second World War US Army manual titled *Field Artillery: Tactical Employment* defines its role:

> Field artillery is a supporting arm. It contributes to the action of the entire force by giving close and continuous fire support to infantry (cavalry) (armored) units and by giving depth to combat by counterbattery fire, fire on hostile reserves, fire to restrict movements in rear areas, and fire to disrupt command agencies.

The same manual also broke down the various classifications of field artillery pieces used by armies during the Second World War as light, medium and heavy. All three categories could include mortars, howitzers and guns.

Medium artillery had a slower rate of fire but greater firepower than light artillery. The weight of its projectile and range made it preferable to light artillery in the counterbattery role. On the downside, its weight and size made it appreciably less mobile than the light artillery. Light and medium artillery pieces were the most numerous towed artillery pieces in all major Second World War armies and typically did most of the firing.

Heavy artillery has a slow rate of fire, great power and long range. It excelled at counterbattery and interdiction fire deep behind enemy lines and extended the neutralizing fire of light and medium artillery pieces. However, it took much longer to emplace and displace compared to light and medium artillery pieces.

A significant disadvantage of heavy artillery is that its barrel life was much shorter than its light and medium counterparts due to higher pressures generated and the resulting bore erosion. The weight and size of the ammunition also proved to be a problem.

The authorized gun crew is entirely satisfactory for servicing this gun. The existing shells and propellants are also entirely satisfactory for completing tasks assigned to this gun.

The gun's springs let it be towed at a speed of 60kph [37mph] on good roads and up to 15–20kph [9–12mph] on bad roads. An average daily range depends on the type of transport. Situations occurred when the gun travelled 250km.

122mm Guns

Soviet industry came up with two versions of a 122mm gun. The first was the almost 8-ton 122mm M1931 (A-19). As with most of the larger Red Army cannons, the weapon had an interrupted screw breech mechanism. It could fire between three and four rounds per minute up to a maximum range of approximately 13 miles. It fired a roughly 55lb HE round with a muzzle velocity of 2,640ft/s.

From 450 to 500 examples of the M1931 (A-19) came down the assembly lines between 1935 and 1939. It had a split trail carriage and rode on large metal spoked wheels that included a suspension system. The carriage design and the spoked metal wheels proved unsatisfactory in use and pushed the Red Army to ask industry for changes.

An improved version of the M1931 (A-19) became the 122mm Gun M1931/37 (A-19). It consisted of the M1931 (A-19) barrel on the more modern carriage of the

---

Infantry Division Artillery Organization

In the 1946 War Department publication titled the *Handbook on USSR Military Forces*, Chapter III, 'Field Organization' is the following extract on their infantry division artillery complement:

> Divisional artillery consists of a mixed field artillery regiment, an anti-tank battalion and an anti-aircraft machine gun company. The mixed artillery regiment includes 998 officers and enlisted men. It is armed with 122mm howitzers and 76mm guns. With the exception of the 122mm howitzers, which are tractor-drawn, and ammunition trucks, the regiment is horse-drawn. Thus, divisional artillery, although it is lighter than that of the US infantry division, is capable of providing close support to the rifle regiments in varying terrain and weather.
>
> The divisional anti-tank battalion consists of headquarters, headquarters battery, three firing batteries; each with four 45mm anti-tank guns and a small train [supply units]. During the last year of the war with Germany, the 45mm anti-tank guns of the anti-tank battalion were often replaced by 57mm anti-tank or 76mm guns ... The divisional anti-aircraft machine-gun company is armed with eighteen 12.7mm anti-aircraft machine guns. It was reintroduced into the rifle division during the summer of 1944.

152mm Howitzer-gun M1937. Rather than having two large metal spoked wheels, it rode on four large rubber tyres, two on either side of the carriage. It also had a suspension system.

Starting in 1939 and continuing into 1946, Soviet industry completed around 2,500 examples of the M1931/39 (A-19). A modified version of the M1931/39 gun provided the weapon for the ISU-122 self-propelled gun and the ISU-2 heavy tank.

152mm Howitzers

In a mirror image of what transpired with the Red Army's 122mm howitzers and guns in the 1930s, Soviet industry partially modernized two pre-First World War 152mm howitzers. These included the 152mm Howitzer M1909 and the 152mm Howitzer M1910.

The upgraded M1909 became the M1909/30 and the M1910 the M1910/37. About 2,500 examples of the former went through a partial modernization and 100 of the latter.

The only major change to both howitzers involved enlarging their chambers to fit a larger propelling charge that increased their range. They retained their original box trails and unsprung wooden spoked wheels. However, some late-production examples of the howitzers featured steel wheels with rubber tyres and a suspension system.

The roughly 3-ton 152mm howitzers had interrupted screw breech mechanisms with a rate of fire of five to six rounds per minute. The maximum range for the howitzers came in at just under 5 miles. The M1909/30 proved to be the most numerous 152mm howitzer in service with the Red Army when the German Army invaded.

The M1909/30 would remain in service with the Red Army in decreasing numbers until the end of the Second World War. The German Army employed captured examples during the conflict and manufactured ammunition for the howitzer.

Post-First World War Howitzers

A replacement for the M1909/30 and the M1910/37 was the 152mm Howitzer M1938 (M-10), with 1,552 examples built between 1939 and 1941. The Red Army ordered production halted upon the German invasion. One reason for its cancellation was its complexity, which created problems in its construction and maintenance issues in the field.

The roughly 4.5-ton M1938 (M-10) howitzer had a modern split trail and rode on four steel wheels with rubber tyres – two on either side of the carriage – with a suspension system. The rate of fire was three to four rounds per minute with a maximum range of around 8 miles. It fired an 88lb HE round at a muzzle velocity of 1,673ft/s. Despite its production ending, those built remained in Red Army service in dwindling numbers until the war ended.

Red Army displeasure with the 152mm Howitzer M1938 (M-10) split-trail carriage led industry to develop a different configuration. As described in the late Ian V. Hogg's book titled *Allied Artillery of World War Two*:

... rather than interfere with production by ordering new designs, they [the Red Army] wisely stayed with what they knew and produced them by the thousands. However, the stresses and strain of war soon told on the M1938 howitzer; putting a 152mm barrel on a lighter carriage had over-stressed it, and by July 1942, there was an urgent need to replace it with a better and stronger design ... the weight came down to 3.5 tons [with the new carriage design], but the equipment was far more reliable, and it went into service as the 152mm howitzer 1943.

The new carriage found itself based on the split-trail carriage of the 122mm Howitzer M1938 (M-10). About 3,000 examples of the M1943 (D-1) rolled out of the factories from 1943, continuing until 1949. The rate of fire was three to four rounds per minute with a maximum range of around 8 miles.

152mm Guns

When the Germans invaded, the oldest 152mm guns in the Red Army (about 150) were the 152mm Gun M1910/30s. These were descended from a pre-First World War cannon labelled the 152mm Siege Gun M1910. Firing a 96lb HE round, the M1910/30 had a muzzle velocity of 2,132ft/s.

The almost 3-ton M1910/30s in their upgraded form featured a muzzle brake and steel wheels with solid rubber rims. The carriage did not have a suspension system. The M1910/30 retained the original box trail. Due to the configuration of the cannon, the carriage and barrel were separate loads.

The pre-Second World War replacement for the M1910/30 in Red Army service was the 152mm Gun M1910/34. It combined the M1910/30's lengthened barrel with the split-trail carriage of the 122mm Gun M1931 (M-19).

The M1910/34 featured a muzzle brake and fired three to four rounds per minute up to a maximum range of about 11 miles. Production took place between 1934 and 1937, with 275 examples completed.

A refined version of the M1910/34 became the 152mm Gun-Howitzer M1937 (ML-20). Instead of the large spoked steel wheels with solid rubber tyres of its predecessor, it featured four large concave steel wheels, two on either side of the split-trail chassis, fitted with pneumatic tires; a modified form of the gun-howitzer armed the SU-152 self-propelled gun.

A 1946 War Department publication lists the roles performed by the 152mm Gun-Howitzer M1937 (ML-20) and the 122mm Gun M1931/37 (A-19) when serving in medium artillery brigades:

> The brigade is used against targets which are beyond the range and capabilities of the light howitzer brigade. Its primary missions are destruction or neutralization of artillery and armored trains [supply formations], neutralization or interdiction of distant targets, destruction of field fortifications, fire reconnaissance of important or exceptionally resistant targets, and destruction of distant minefields.

The M1937's (ML-20) most significant improvement over the M1910/34 was that it travelled in one piece. Between 1937 and 1947, a total of 6,884 examples came off the assembly line. It fired a 96lb HE round with a muzzle velocity of 2,149ft/s.

In service, the M1937 (ML-20) proved reliable and easy to maintain. One of its key advantages was that it outranged its German counterparts. It also proved to be lighter and more cost-effective to build.

A Tracked Carriage

One of the larger towed 152mm artillery pieces fielded by the Red Army was the 152mm Gun M1935 (Br-2). Rather than a wheeled carriage, the cannon rode on an unpowered tracked carriage. Gun and tracked carriage together weighed about 20 tons.

Like the M1910/34, the carriage and barrel of the M1935 (Br-2) were towed separately. The rate of fire was less than a round per minute. The maximum range came to around 15 miles. It fired a 108lb HE round with a muzzle velocity of 2,149ft/s. Only thirty-seven of these were built, with surviving examples remaining in use throughout the Second World War.

Another Red Army artillery piece that also rode on the same unpowered tracked carriage as the 152mm Gun M1935 (Br-2) was the 203mm Howitzer M1931 (B-4). Soviet industry produced 871 examples from 1932 to 1942. It fired a 217lb HE round.

The roughly 39,000lb M1931 (B-4) could fire around one round every four minutes to a maximum range of approximately 11 miles. Some would see service in the direct fire mode during the Red Army seizure of Berlin, which took place during April and May 1945.

Self-Propelled Rocket-Launchers

The artillery branch of the Red Army commissioned a Soviet research institute in June 1938 to develop a ground-to-ground rocket based on an existing Red Air Force air-to-ground rocket. Testing began the same year, and by the time of the German invasion the Red Army had forty examples of a truck-mounted rocket-launcher assembly in service. Each rocket-launcher assembly came with sixteen HE warhead-armed rockets with a range of about 6 miles.

The early success of the rocket-armed trucks, designated the BM-13, led to an order for many more. As time went on, the rockets themselves began appearing in ever-larger sizes, and these included 82mm, 132mm, 280mm and up to 300mm. At the 300mm size, the rocket had a 64lb HE warhead and a range of almost 3 miles. Obviously the larger the rocket, the fewer the trucks could transport.

Because the rocket-launcher assemblies were nothing but a simple metal framework, factories lacking the skill and infrastructure to build conventional towed artillery pieces could still contribute to the war effort.

Some rocket-launcher assemblies saw use only as static ground platforms. Sources suggest that approximately 10,000 examples of the mobile rocket-launchers came down the Soviet assembly lines during the Second World War, with millions of rockets constructed.

The original three-axle trucks used by the Red Army were Soviet industry copies of 1930s-era Ford Motor commercial trucks. Eventually, more modern and capable Lend-Lease trucks with better off-road mobility became the rocket-launchers' preferred platform, resulting in the designation BM-13N. The most common chassis for the rocket-launchers was the American-designed and built three-axle 2.5-ton 6×6 Studebaker truck.

Besides trucks, the rocket-launchers also went onto some unarmoured tracked prime movers, including the turretless chassis of two light tanks. This variant allowed the crews to move their vehicles closer to the enemy's front lines than was possible with the unarmoured trucks.

Not as accurate as conventional artillery pieces, rocket-launchers could still deliver an impressive amount of fire onto unprotected area targets in minutes. Due to their very identifiable launch signature, the launchers had to retire quickly from their firing locations in order to avoid enemy counterbattery fire. Besides a lack of accuracy, another rocket-launcher disadvantage was a slow reload time.

The Soviet soldiers nicknamed the vehicle-mounted rocket-launcher the 'Katyusha' from a then-popular wartime song about a young girl who missed her soldier lover. The German soldiers who endured a bombardment by the rocket-launchers nicknamed them 'Stalin's Organ' for two reasons: one, the Soviet leader had compared the launcher assemblies to a pipe organ; and two, the unmistakable and distinctive wailing sound of the rocket motors when fired.

The Biggest Mortar

It may not be clear to the reader why the 160mm mortar is broken out in Chapter Five, when all other mortars including the 120mm mentioned below are in Chapter One.

The largest mortar placed into service by the Red Army received the label of 160mm Mortar M1943, with about 500 examples built. Weighing in at a little over a ton, it rode on pneumatic tyres and was moved by wheeled or tracked vehicles. It is also referred to as the MT-13, with the letters 'MT' standing for 'Mortar Teverovskiy'. The latter was the name of the head of the weapon's design group.

Due to the 10ft height of the 160mm mortar tube when erected and the weight of its 90lb bombs, it was a breech-loaded weapon, in contrast to all the Red Army's smaller-calibre mortars that were muzzle-loaded. It had a three round per minute rate of fire with a maximum range of about 3 miles.

Anti-Aircraft Guns

Soviet industry provided the Red Army with a range of anti-aircraft guns. The smallest was the Tokarev 4M Model 1931. It consisted of a pedestal mount with four 7.62mm Maxim water-cooled machine guns and was mounted on a truck or a static site due to its weight. Its primary target was low-flying ground-attack aircraft as it lacked the effective range to engage aircraft at higher altitudes.

Next up was the 25mm Automatic Air Defence Gun Model 1940 (72-K). It rode on a four-wheel trailer with a combined weight of 2,670lb. Copied from a Swedish Bofors-designed anti-aircraft gun, it fired 240 rounds per minute to a maximum ceiling of around 6,500ft. The production of the weapon did not ramp up until 1943, with about 5,000 completed by the war's end.

Soviet industry also built the 37mm Automatic Air Defence Gun Model 1939 (61-K) based on the Bofors 40mm anti-aircraft gun that had first appeared in 1934. With almost all its artillery pieces, the Red Army preferred using ammunition

One-of-a-Kind Organization

The Red Army's senior leadership noticed a severe problem while reviewing the performance of its infantry divisions during the opening stages of the German invasion. Their commanding officers failed to use their organic artillery assets effectively. Adding to the problem was a lack of suitable radios at the divisional level and the poor educational levels of Red Army soldiers from rural areas.

To rectify this problem, the Red Army senior leadership decided in October 1942 to concentrate most of their artillery pieces and support equipment as well as better-educated talent into specialized 'artillery divisions'. No other major army would duplicate this organizational structure.

Artillery divisions came under the oversight of army-level commands, or the Soviet high command known as 'Stavka' formed on 23 June 1941. These higher-level commands allocated the artillery divisions to support large-scale infantry and armoured division operations based on requirements.

Each artillery division usually consisted of four artillery brigades. Between them, they had 168 towed artillery pieces and 80 120mm mortars. The Red Army would also go on to form independent artillery regiments and brigades. The latter typically consisted of two to four artillery regiments.

Eventually the Red Army formed artillery corps headquarter units (which came under the supervision of field armies) to oversee artillery divisions. In April 1943, the Red Army decided to convert most of its artillery divisions into a new type of division called 'Breakthrough Artillery Divisions'. These had a 152mm howitzer and a 203mm howitzer brigade added. Their inventory rose to 248 towed artillery pieces and 108 120mm mortars.

In a further subdivision of its artillery inventory, in June 1943 the Red Army formed the first of two 'Heavy Gun Artillery Divisions'. Each consisted of four brigades with a combined total of 144 examples of the 152mm Gun-Howitzer. One of the Red Army's artillery divisions became a 'Gun Artillery Division' with 48 76mm guns and 108 of the 152mm gun-howitzers.

In September 1944, the Red Army formed more breakthrough artillery divisions featuring a new organization (TO&E) table. Each had 188 towed artillery pieces and 140 mortars (108 of the 120mm mortar and 32 new 160mm mortars). In addition, the 1944 TO&E provided for thirty-six truck-mounted rocket-launchers. Eventually the Red Army would also form both rocket-launcher and anti-aircraft divisions.

already in production (such as the 37mm round) rather than introducing new sizes that would impose a burden on its already strained logistical system.

In Red Army service, the 4,600lb 37mm anti-aircraft gun had a muzzle velocity of 2,900ft/s, firing 160 to 170 rounds per minute. The maximum ceiling was around 16,000ft. Soviet industry built approximately 20,000 examples during the Second World War.

The Problem of Hitting the Target

From a War Department manual dated August 1940 and concerning anti-aircraft artillery is the following passage on the difficulty of hitting an aircraft:

In its essential features, the problem of firing at an airplane is the same as firing at any moving land or water target. In its details, it is more complex due to the greater speed of the airplane and its ability to move in three dimensions. In all cases, it is desired to make the projectile meet the target at some point in space. In anti-aircraft-gun firing, the small, vulnerable area presented by an airplane target makes it desirable to cause the projectile to burst, not upon impact as with seacoast artillery, but on or just short of the expected position of the target in order to increase the probability of hitting. The elementary problem consists of predicting the future location of the target on the basis of its behavior during some interval of time just prior to the prediction, and calculating data necessary to pass a trajectory through this point.

In the 2 December 1943 issue of *Tactical and Technical Trends* is the following passage from an article titled 'Russian Anti-Aircraft Methods':

... enemy air raids were characterized by concentrated attacks on small targets. Dozens of Ju planes [Ju-87 Stuka dive-bombers], one after another, made diving attacks on specific objectives, dropping their bombs on small areas ... great endurance is required of the anti-aircraft crews.

Intensive counterfire is necessary to prevent the success of concentrated enemy raids. In combating an air attack, our gun crews fired long salvoes at a definite point where the German planes went into their dives. If the leading plane did succeed in getting through the wall of fire and dropped its bombs, the following planes were sure to get into the zone of fire. Following these tactics, one of our batteries brought down three bombers during the first day.

For dealing with enemy aircraft at higher altitudes, Soviet industry came up with the 76.2mm Anti-Aircraft Gun Model 1931 (3-K) and an improved model with a different carriage design labelled the Model 1938 (3-K). Of the former, industry built 3,821 examples, and of the latter 960 examples. The roughly 5-ton weapon had a muzzle velocity of 2,667ft/s, a rate of fire of between ten and twenty rounds per minute and a maximum ceiling of about 31,000ft.

The Red Army's replacement for its 76.2mm anti-aircraft guns was a scaled-up version labelled the 85mm Anti-Aircraft Gun Model 1939 (52-K). The weapon also weighed about 5 tons and fired ten to twelve rounds per minute at a muzzle velocity of 2,598ft/s. The maximum ceiling came in at about 51,000ft, but with an effective altitude of approximately 30,000ft.

An upgraded Model 1939 (52-K), with an enlarged chamber for a larger cartridge case, became the Model 1944 (KS-18). Both versions of the 85mm anti-aircraft guns sported a muzzle brake, but the 76.2mm anti-aircraft guns did not.

Anti-Aircraft Division Organization

In a 1946 War Department publication titled *Handbook on USSR Military Forces*, Chapter III, 'Field Organization' is an extract on their anti-aircraft formations:

> The anti-aircraft artillery division consists of three 37mm anti-aircraft automatic weapons regiments, an 85mm gun regiment, and divisional troops. The 85mm gun regiment is approximately equal in personnel and armament to the US 90mm gun battalion. The 37mm anti-aircraft automatic weapons regiment is approximately equal to half a US anti-aircraft automatic weapons battalion. Thus, the Red Army anti-aircraft division corresponds roughly to a US automatic anti-aircraft weapons group.
>
> One anti-aircraft artillery division is generally assigned to each operational Army and one or more to each Army Group (Front). In addition to their primary mission of anti-aircraft defense of important installations and troop concentrations, anti-aircraft artillery units are used for anti-tank defense, support of ground troops by direct fire against targets whose destruction requires high-velocity fire, and less often for indirect fire against general ground targets.

Soviet industry completed approximately 6,000 examples of the 85mm anti-aircraft gun by 1945. The Germans thought highly of the gun and quickly adopted captured examples into service.

In addition to the Red Army's dedicated anti-tank guns, anti-aircraft guns became improvised anti-tank guns. In the 18 June 1942 War Department publication titled *Tactical and Technical Trends* there is a passage taken from *Red Star*, a Soviet newspaper, on the Red Army's employment of anti-aircraft guns:

> In the first six months of the war, Red Army anti-aircraft artillery fired in self-defence at enemy tanks which broke through to the battery positions. Gradually, however, the anti-aircraft artillery became an organic part of the anti-tank defensive system. In numerous instances, Russian anti-aircraft guns have successfully repulsed attacks of large tank units.

(**Opposite, above**) A wartime image of two Red Army 45mm Anti-Tank Guns M1937. The weapon's factory-assigned number was 53-K. Nicknamed the 'Little Forty-Five', it entered Red Army service in 1938. It fired a one-piece (fixed) round, powerful enough to deal with enemy tanks in the summer of 1941. The following year it was obsolete as the Germans had up-armoured their tanks. When production ended in 1943, Soviet industry had built approximately 37,000 examples of the 45mm anti-tank gun. (*Author's collection*)

(**Opposite, below**) To deal with the up-armoured German tanks in 1942, Soviet industry developed a modified version of the 45mm Anti-Tank Gun M1937. The new version had a longer barrel that increased its muzzle velocity and armour penetration capabilities. That longer-barrelled model seen here became the 45mm Anti-Tank Gun M1942 with the factory designation M-42. In addition to the new barrel, the weapon's gun shield was thickened. About 10,000 examples were produced between 1942 and 1945. (*Dreamstime*)

(**Opposite, above**) In 1940 there arose a belief that the German Army would field more thickly-armoured tanks. In response, the Red Army took into service the 57mm Anti-Tank Gun Model 1941 (ZiS-2), which fired fixed rounds. However, following the German invasion, it was clear that the gun was not needed and production concluded in December 1941. When more thickly-armoured German tanks finally appeared, in June 1943 the Model 1941 was put back into production as the Model M1943 pictured here. It retained the original factory number. (*PICRYL*)

(**Above**) In this picture we see a Red Army 76mm Divisional Gun M1902/30. It was a modernized version of the 76mm Divisional Gun M1902 with a longer barrel. Both guns were nicknamed 'the 3-incher' by artillerymen. The cannons fired a fixed round and lasted in service with the Red Army into the Second World War. Despite upgrades, the M1902/30 retained an obsolete one-piece pole trail that limited elevation. A hole was cut into the pole trail by industry to raise the elevation by a few degrees. (*Dreamstime*)

(**Opposite, below**) The Red Army replacement for the 76mm Divisional Gun M1902/30 was the the 76mm Divisional Gun M1936 with factory code F-22. Production began in 1937 and continued until 1939, with around 3,000 examples built. Besides indirect fire, the M1936 could perform as a direct-fire anti-tank weapon. The Red Army also tasked industry with making it capable of sufficient elevation for an anti-aircraft role. (*Dreamstime*)

(**Above**) Pictured here is a 76mm Divisional Gun M1939 (USV). Like its predecessor the F-22, it had a modern split-trail carriage. It differed from other weapons as its recoil mechanism was no longer in one piece under the barrel. Instead it consisted of two separate pieces: a hydraulic recoil buffer on top of the barrel and a hydro-pneumatic recuperator under the barrel. This arrangement provided improved cooling during prolonged firing. Production began in 1939 and ended in 1940 before the German invasion. (*PICRYL*)

(**Opposite, above**) Upon the German invasion, Marshal Grigory Kulick (in charge of the Red Army's artillery branch) ordered that production of the 76mm Divisional Gun M1939 (USV) should restart. Vasiliy G. Grabin, an artillery designer, had secretly come up with a more simplified 76mm anti-tank gun configuration in 1940. It incorporated the split-trail carriage of the 57mm Anti-Tank Gun ZiS-2 with the barrel of the USV fitted with a muzzle brake. Eventually the Red Army embraced the weapon seen here, which entered into series production as the 76mm Divisional Gun M1942 (ZiS-3). (*Dreamstime*)

(**Below**) Battlefield success of the 76mm Divisional Gun M1942 (ZiS-3) can be gauged by the fact that Soviet industry built approximately 100,000 examples between 1941 and 1945. The gun weighed about 2,500lb, which allowed it to be manoeuvred around the battlefield for short distances by human muscle power, as seen here in this wartime image. Befitting its primary role as an anti-tank gun, it fired fixed rounds and had a semi-automatic breechblock mechanism. (*Author's collection*)

(**Above**) Soviet industry began development work on a towed 107mm gun in late 1938 that eventually became the 107mm Divisional Gun M1940 (M-60) pictured here. Instead of firing a fixed round and having a semi-automatic breechblock mechanism, the M-60 fired separately-loaded rounds and had an interrupted screw breechblock mechanism. Soviet industry lacked the wartime ability to build semi-automatic breechblocks for larger-calibre artillery pieces. Shortly after the German invasion, the Red Army cancelled the M-60 due to its cost, complexity and unresolved design issues. (*PICRYL*)

(**Opposite, above**) As with other armies' artillery pieces, to deal with ever more thickly-armoured tanks, those of the Red Army became progressively larger and heavier as the war went on. An example of that process is seen here: the roughly 2-ton 85mm Divisional Gun with the factory code D-44. Reflecting its primary role as an anti-tank gun, it fired fixed rounds. Note that the weapon's compact recoil system is located entirely behind its gun shield. (*Dreamstime*)

(**Opposite, below**) Pushing the size and weight limits of what a towed anti-tank gun could have, in the closing stages of the war the Red Army fielded the approximately 4-ton 100mm Field Gun M1944. It bore the factory code BS-3. The weapon itself was derived from a naval gun. Like the 85mm Divisional Gun, the 100mm Field Gun M1944 fired fixed rounds as seen in the loader's hands in this image. In addition to AP rounds, the weapon fired an HE-FRAG round in the indirect-fire mode to a distance of around 12 miles. (*Author's collection*)

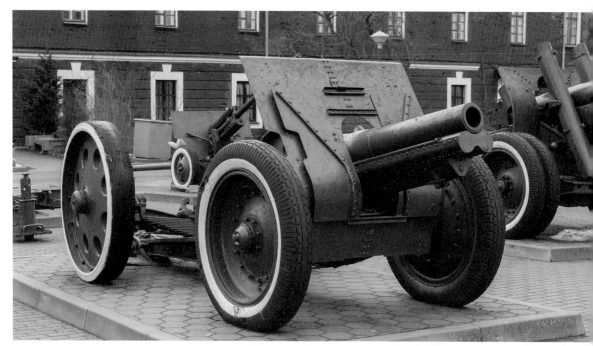

The standard divisional howitzer for the Imperial Russian Army and the Red Army was 122mm in calibre. The original pre-First World War version, the 122mm Howitzer M1910, lasted until the Second World War. A modernized version, with rubber wheels for towing by prime movers is seen here. It was assigned the designation 122mm Howitzer M1920/30. Like other large-calibre Red Army artillery pieces, it fired separately-loading rounds and had an interrupted screw breechblock mechanism. (*Dreamstime*)

By the 1930s the Red Army knew that all its pre-First World War-designed artillery pieces such as the 122mm Howitzer M1910 were obsolete. Therefore, it tasked industry with development of a new 122mm howitzer. The first attempt resulted in eight examples referred to as the 122mm Howitzer M1934. These proved a dead end and led to the subsequent design, manufacture and fielding of the 122mm Howitzer M1938 (M-30) pictured here. In its firing mode, it weighed about 3 tons. (*Dreamstime*)

A Red Army sentry guards a battery of 122mm Howitzers M1938 (M-30). Like other replacement weapons, the choice of its calibre was influenced by available stocks of ammunition. At one point a 105mm artillery piece was under consideration. However, as Soviet industry had no experience in its design and manufacturing, it faded from consideration. Due to its interrupted screw breechblock mechanism and separately-loaded ammunition, the 122mm Howitzer M1938's rate of fire was only five to six rounds per minute. (*Author's collection*)

(**Above**) On display here is a 122mm Gun M1931/37 (A-19), the modernized version of the 122mm Gun M1931 (A-19). Whereas its predecessor had rubber-rimmed metal-spoked wheels, the 8-ton M1931/37 (A-19) had four large pneumatic tyres, with two on either side of the carriage. These allowed for towing at higher speeds. The two near-vertical cylinders on either side of the barrel are hydro-pneumatic equilibrators to balance the cannon's long, heavy barrel. These allowed the barrel to be easily elevated or depressed by use of a hand wheel. (*Dreamstime*)

(**Opposite, above**) Shown here is the 152mm Howitzer M1938 (M-10). It was the intended replacement for the Red Army's pre-First World War 152mm Howitzer M1909 and the slightly-improved 152mm Howitzer M1910. Unlike its predecessors that rode on metal-rimmed wooden-spoked wheels, the M-10 had four large pneumatic tyres, two on either side of the carriage. However, as happened to the 107mm Divisional Gun M1940 (M-60), the Red Army cancelled further production of the M-10 following the German invasion due to the weapon's complexity and cost. (*PICRYL*)

(**Opposite, below**) Soviet industry, to keep costs down and increase production volume, combined features of various artillery pieces to make new cannons. An example is the 152mm Howitzer M1943 (D-1) pictured here. Its barrel came from the 152mm Howitzer M1938 (M-10) with a large muzzle brake fitted to reduce recoil forces. The barrel is mounted on a modified carriage from the 122mm Howitzer M1938 (M-30). With a crew of eight, the 4-ton cannon could fire between three to four rounds per minute to a maximum range of about 8 miles. (*Dreamstime*)

As the Red Army fought in 1945 to take urban centres of Eastern and Central Europe, it was not uncommon to see large artillery pieces such as the 152mm Gun M1910/34 pictured here pressed into the direct-fire mode. This especially occurred when taking on enemy strongpoints established in multi-storey buildings. The M1910/34's design could be traced back to the Russian Imperial Army's 152mm Siege Gun M1910. The cannon weighed more than 8 tons and had a maximum range of about 11 miles. (*Author's collection*)

The upgraded replacement for the 152mm Gun M1910/34 was the 152mm Howitzer Gun M1937 (ML-20) pictured here. Like its predecessor, the ML-20 came with a massive multi-slotted muzzle brake. When prepared for transport, the cannon's long barrel was normally retracted onto its carriage to prevent it from striking the ground when travelling over uneven terrain. The carriage itself was from the 122mm Gun M1931/37 (A-19). As with other large-calibre artillery pieces, its rate of fire ranged from three to four rounds per minute. (*Dreamstime*)

Shown here is the 203mm Howitzer M1931 (B-4). Rather than having a wheeled chassis, the cannon sat on an unpowered tracked chassis that could be towed over short distances by a tracked prime mover. The cannon was designed in 1931 and placed into production the following year, with approximately 800 examples completed by October 1941. Due to the weight and size of its ammunition, the cannon's rate of fire was about one round every four minutes. The gun had a crew of fifteen men and could hurl an HE round out to a range of around 11 miles. (*Dreamstime*)

(**Above**) Mounted on the same unpowered tracked carriage as the M1931 (B-4) is the 20-ton 152mm Gun M1935 (Br-2). For transport over longer distances, the barrel was removed from its carriage and transported separately. The barrel was then remounted on its carriage at their destination. The maximum range was about 17 miles. Sources suggest that only thirty-seven examples of the Br-2 came off the factory floor. (*Dreamstime*)

(**Opposite, above**) A third Red Army artillery piece mounted on the same unpowered tracked carriage as the 152mm Gun M1935 (Br-2) and the 203mm Howitzer M1931 (B-4) was the 280mm Mortar M1939 (Br-5) seen here. Looking much like the B-4, its shorter breech-loaded barrel is the only major external difference. Only forty-seven examples came off the assembly line between 1939 and 1940. The Br-5 fired an anti-concrete round weighing 542lb with a 99lb projectile warhead out to a maximum range of around 6 miles. Like the B-4, its fifteen-man crew could only fire one round every four minutes. (*Dreamstime*)

(**Opposite, below**) The Red Navy had little to do during the Second World War. To make productive use of its weaponry, some of its larger guns were converted into railroad artillery pieces. This example bore the designation TM-1-180, designed around 180mm guns that had armed Red Navy cruisers. To allow the gun 360 degrees of traverse, the carriage had large stabilizing jacks which are shown in its travelling configuration stored alongside the lower portion of a custom railroad car. (*Dreamstime*)

(**Above**) Seen here at the former US Army Ordnance Museum is a Red Army 160mm Mortar 1943, a design introduced into service in early 1944. Around 500 of these were constructed by 1945. Production for the Soviet Army continued after the war. It has an almost 10ft-long barrel and weighs more than 1 ton. It required a wheeled vehicle to move it into and out of firing positions. Due to its size, it was not muzzle-loaded like most mortars but breech-loaded. Its crew could fire a 90lb HE round out to a maximum range of about 3 miles, with a rate of fire of around three rounds per minute. (*PICRYL*)

(**Opposite, below**) In the late 1930s a Soviet research institute began modifying an existing fin-stabilized aircraft air-to-ground rocket for employment as a truck-mounted surface-to-surface rocket. In its initial configuration the rocket-launcher assembly appeared in a transverse configuration (firing to the vehicle's side) on a Russian-built 6 × 6 truck chassis. That arrangement did not work well, and the rocket-launcher assembly was repositioned to fire over the cab of a 6 × 6 truck as pictured here. In that configuration it became the BM-13. When in its firing position, stabilizing jacks at the rear corners of the chassis were extended. (*Dreamstime*)

(**Above**) To improve off-road mobility of its rocket-launcher assemblies, the Red Army tried mounting them on unarmoured full-tracked artillery-towing tractors. As the tractors were slow and possessed a limited range, the Red Army rethought the idea and decided to mount some of their rocket-launcher assemblies on surplus turretless light tanks such as the T-40 and the T-60 pictured here. Besides having a longer operational range, they offered the crew a degree of protection from enemy counterbattery fire. (*Dreamstime*)

(**Opposite, above**) In their final iteration pictured here, Soviet-built rocket-launcher assemblies were mounted on American-designed and built 6 × 6 trucks supplied under Lend-Lease. These vehicles possessed far superior on-road and off-road mobility than the earlier Russian-built 6 × 6 trucks. The example pictured here was labelled the BM-13N and made up about half the Red Army's inventory of rocket-launching trucks by the end of the Second World War. Modified rocket-launcher assemblies also went onto Red Army naval vessels as well as armoured trains. (*Author's collection*)

(**Opposite, below**) Seen here on the roof of a multi-storey building is the Tokarev 4M Model 1931 quadruple anti-aircraft mount. It consisted of four water-cooled 7.62mm M1910/30 medium machine guns fitted onto a heavy pedestal mount, which could also go into the cargo bay of 6 × 6 trucks. Due to its relatively limited effective ceiling and rifle-calibre ammunition, it posed a threat only to very low-flying and poorly-armoured aircraft. As more heavily-armoured German ground-attack aircraft began appearing in 1942, its effectiveness was reduced. (*Author's collection*)

(**Above**) The Red Army was well aware of the shortcomings of its 7.62mm machine guns in the anti-aircraft role. It therefore had Soviet industry come up with the 25mm Anti-Aircraft Gun M1940 (72-K) pictured here. The weapon weighed just over 1 ton and was copied from a Swedish design. It had a rate of fire of approximately 240 rounds per minute. The rounds were loaded manually into the weapon in six-round clips. The maximum effective ceiling for the rounds came in at just under 8,000ft. Around 2,500 examples of the 72-K were built during the Second World War. (*PICRYL*)

Another anti-aircraft gun that entered Red Army service before the German invasion was the 37mm Automatic Air Defence Gun M1939 (61-K) pictured here. Like the 25mm Anti-Aircraft Gun M1940 (72-K), the 61-K was based on a Swedish design, hence resembling the famous Bofors 40mm anti-aircraft gun. It was fed by manually-loaded five-round clips and had a maximum effective ceiling of 13,000ft. (*Author's collection*)

For engaging enemy bombers at higher altitudes, the Red Army fielded the 76mm Air Defence Gun M1931 (3-K), a captured example of which is pictured here in Finnish Army service. Broadly based on the design of a British 76mm anti aircraft gun, the 3-K weighed about 4 tons in firing order and around 5 tons in travelling order. It had a crew of ten men, who could attain a firing rate of between ten and twenty rounds per minute. It had a maximum effective ceiling of about 31,000ft. An upgraded model was the 76mm Air Defence Gun M1938. (*SA-Kuva*)

The replacement for the 76mm Air Defence Gun M1931/M1938 (3-K) in Red Army service was the roughly 5-ton 85mm Air Defence Gun M1939 (52-K), followed by an identical later version firing a more powerful 85m round designated the Model 1944 (KS-18). The latter appears here with its stabilizing outriggers in position. Unlike the 76mm Air Defence Gun M1931 (3-K) and upgraded 76mm Air Defence Gun M1938 (3-K), both models of the 85mm anti-aircraft gun featured muzzle brakes. (*Dreamstime*)

During a historical demonstration, Russian re-enactors dressed in reproduction Red Army uniforms man an 85mm Air Defence Gun Model 1944 (KS-18). It had a rate of fire of between ten and twelve rounds per minute and a maximum effective ceiling of around 35,000ft. Captured examples were placed into service by the German military, with some eventually rebored to fire the standard German 88mm round. (*Dreamstime*)

Chapter Six

Miscellaneous Armoured Fighting Vehicles

The Red Army decided in the early 1930s that it needed self-propelled artillery, so its artillery branch subsequently came up with prototypes of varying sizes and armaments. Only two went into limited production: the SU-5-2 and the BT-7A.

The SU-5-2 consisted of a short-barrelled 122m howitzer mounted in a fixed, open-topped, forward-firing position on the modified T-26 light tank chassis. The prefix letters 'SU' are the abbreviation in the Russian language for the words 'self-propelled' or 'mechanized'.

The BT-7A consisted of a 76.2mm howitzer in an oversized turret with 360 degrees of traverse, mounted on a BT-7 light tank chassis. The suffix letter 'A' stands for artillery in the Russian language. Like the SU-5-2, the BT-7A had no indirect fire capability.

Somewhere between 130 and 160 examples of the BT-7A came off the assembly lines between 1936 and 1938. All would be lost in the summer of 1941 in trying to stem the German invasion.

SU-76 Series

Following the terrible tank losses suffered by the Red Army in 1941, whatever resources it could amass were dedicated to replacing them as quickly as possible. There was little industrial capacity remaining to design and build specialized vehicles such as self-propelled guns. Nevertheless, by the spring of 1942, the Red Army recognized a pressing need for a dedicated infantry support vehicle.

Strangely enough, it would be the armour branch of the Red Army and not the artillery branch that initiated the development of self-propelled guns, the first of which would acquire the label of the light SU-76. A crew of three men serviced the open-topped fixed forward-firing 76.2mm field gun, which had limited traverse and elevation.

The approximately 11 ton SU-76 rode on the modified chassis of the twin gasoline-engine-powered T-70 light tank. Unlike the rear-hull engines of the T-70, the SU-76 had its engines mounted in the front hull.

Powertrain issues that plagued early examples of the T-70 did the same to the SU-76. With the addition of a design fix, both vehicles had the suffix letter 'M' added to their designations, this standing for 'modernized'. Eventually all the early-production SU-76s went back to the factory for upgrading into the SU-76M configuration.

Modifying Captured Enemy Tanks

Such was the demand for self-propelled guns in early 1943 due to powertrain problems with the early-production SU-76 that Red Army leadership directed Soviet industry to convert captured Panzer III medium tanks and their variants into turretless 76.2mm gun-armed self-propelled guns for its own use.

This strange combination of German and Soviet-built components received the designation SU-76i, the suffix letter 'i' being the Russian abbreviation for the word 'foreign'. Unlike the SU-76 series, the SU-76i provided its gun crew with overhead protection.

At least 200 examples of the SU-76i came down the assembly lines by the end of 1943. Twenty of those were configured as command vehicles. The SU-76i would remain in service until early 1944 when the supply of spare parts was exhausted.

In addition to the SU-76i, there also appeared in 1942 what the Red Army referred to as the SG-122. It consisted of a Red Army 122mm howitzer mounted onto the modified chassis of the Panzer III medium tank and its variants. The gun of the SG-122 resided in an armoured casemate at the front of the vehicle's hull with limited traverse and elevation.

Only twenty examples of the SG-122 are reported to have been built, not counting the single pre-production pilot vehicle. They would see action in 1943, with some lost to enemy fire. The factory's inability to acquire a sufficient number of captured Panzer III tanks and variants led to the SG-122 programme's termination in 1943.

The SU-76 series began coming off the assembly lines in December 1942. By the time production of the SU-76 concluded at the war's end, a total of 12,671 examples had entered the Red Army inventory, making it the second most-produced Soviet-built armoured vehicle after the T-34 series.

In the Field

Thinly-armoured, the open-topped SU-76 series proved vulnerable to almost every enemy weapon it encountered on the battlefield. The maximum armour thickness on the front of the vehicle topped out at 35mm.

Reflecting its limitations, the SU-76 found itself generally reserved for the infantry support role, with a secondary anti-tank role. The crews of the SU-76 series were well aware of their vehicle's shortcomings and nicknamed it 'the Bitch'.

In an article titled 'Self-Propelled Guns in the Offensive' written by a Red Army general in the February 1945 edition of the *Field Artillery Journal* is the following passage:

Just before the [Red Army] artillery ceased firing, these SP [self-propelled] guns left their concealed positions to join the infantry, which had already raced into action. Our field artillery has seriously disabled the enemy fire system and pinned the Germans to the ground. But when the [Red Army artillery] fire was shifted deeper into the German defences, a number of machine-gun nests and a gun on the left flank renewed their activities. That was when the self-propelled guns played their part. Machines under Lieutenants Seryuk and Petrov made short work of the gun, while the remainder dealt with the machine guns, crushing them with their tracks. Our gunners used their ammunition sparely, for it is not easy to replenish supplies during battles.

Anti-Aircraft Variant

To protect its tank units from German ground-attack aircraft, the Red Army had Soviet industry reconfigure the SU-76 to mount a 37mm anti-aircraft gun in an open-topped 360-degree rotating turret at the rear of the vehicle chassis. In this new configuration, the vehicle became the ZSU-37, the prefix letters 'ZSU' being the Russian abbreviation for 'self-propelled anti-aircraft gun'.

Before production of the ZSU-37 received authorization in 1944, the Red Army decided to employ the upgraded SU-76M chassis. In service use, the slow turret traverse speed of the ZSU-37 made it difficult for its crews to engage fast-moving aircraft. Only a few hundred examples of the ZSU-37 came out of the factory doors.

SU-122

The Red Army approved in the summer of 1942 plans to develop a medium self-propelled gun. Based on the chassis of the T-34 series, its armament was a 122mm howitzer in a front hull armoured casemate with limited traverse and elevation. The vehicle became the SU-122 and started coming off assembly lines in December 1942, the same month as the SU-76 series.

The SU-122 had a four-man crew protected by a maximum frontal armour thickness of 45mm. Due to the size and weight of the main gun rounds, the projectile and propellant were loaded into the breech separately, limiting the vehicle's rate of fire to two rounds per minute. The SU-122 had authorized onboard stowage for forty rounds.

The Reason for Self-Propelled Guns

The SU-76 series, like other turretless self-propelled guns that followed it into Red Army service, were generally employed as direct-fire artillery pieces to take on enemy defensive positions, tanks and other armoured fighting vehicles. They were, in effect, surrogate tanks cheaper and easier to build than turreted vehicles.

By eliminating a turret on an existing chassis, Soviet industry could mount much larger weapons. This was the same train of thought that the German Army followed by producing a series of turretless assault guns based on the chassis of the Panzer III. Encounters with the German assault guns had greatly impressed the Red Army and helped it to embrace the same concept.

Due to the limited elevation of its main gun, the SU-122 primarily fired its 122mm howitzer in direct-fire mode. However, if called upon, it could also take part in indirect fire. An example appears in the book titled *Panzer Destroyer: Memoirs of a Red Army Tank Commander* by Vasiliy Krysov. At one point in the war, he commanded a platoon of SU-122s and recalled: 'Several minutes later at the command of the regiment commander, we joined the artillery preparation, firing on previously assigned and registered targets. Here at the Kursk salient [June 1943], my first experience with indirect fire from covered positions.'

The limited effective range of the SU-122 when engaging enemy tanks led to a halt on SU-122 production in mid-1943. Another reason was that more effective self-propelled guns began entering Red Army service. Total production of the 33-ton SU-122 amounted to 1,148 vehicles.

SU-152

The Red Army replacement for the KV-2 proved to be the SU-152 armed with a 152mm artillery howitzer. It rode on the chassis of the KV-1S heavy tank. Unlike the KV-2 with its 152mm howitzer residing in a 360-degree rotating turret, the SU-152 howitzer went into an armoured casemate in the vehicle's front with limited traverse and elevation.

The five-man SU-152 starting coming off the assembly lines in March 1943, with the first units equipped with the vehicle forming two months later. The 50-ton SU-152 had a maximum armour thickness on the front hull of 60mm, leaving it vulnerable to fire from late-war German tanks and anti-tank guns.

Due to the size and weight of its two-piece main gun rounds, the SU-152 had authorized stowage for only twenty rounds. The time to load the separately-loaded shell and charge components of heavy rounds restricted the rate of fire to only two rounds per minute.

When originally conceived, the SU-152's role was the destruction of enemy defensive works; hence the vehicle had only an HE round and no AP rounds. The advent of the German Tiger 1 pushed the SU-152 into the secondary role of an anti-tank vehicle. Fortunately, its HE rounds' blast effect could destroy German tanks like the Tiger and the Panther, earning it the unofficial nickname of 'the animal hunter'.

The Red Army halted production of the SU-152 in late 1943. By that time, Soviet industry had completed 704 examples. Its battlefield success prompted the Red Army to continue the development of turretless self-propelled guns.

A New Chassis

With the production run of the SU-152 coming to an end, the Red Army began looking at using the new IS-2 heavy tank chassis as a platform on which to mount a 152mm howitzer. That five-man turretless vehicle became the ISU-152. The letter 'I' added to the vehicle's prefix meant that it rode on the chassis of the IS-2 heavy tank. In the English language, the letter 'I' in ISU-152 appears as the letter 'J'.

Due to a shortage of 152mm howitzers, Soviet industry also adopted a 122mm gun (the same that went into the IS-2) to fit onto the ISU-152 turretless chassis. In this configuration, the vehicle became the ISU-122. The ISU-152 had authorized stowage for twenty separately-loaded rounds; the ISU-122 had room for thirty separately-loaded rounds.

From the book *Panzer Killers: Anti-Tank Warfare on the Eastern Front*, a Red Army officer recalled:

> The JSU-152 had a separate load of ammunition. The shell weighed 48 kilograms [106lb], and the casing [cartridge case] weighed 16–20 kilograms [35–44lb] – more brass and less cardboard. For the loader, this demanded unbelievably hard work. We sought to pick guys of a corresponding build – no taller than 160 centimetres [5ft], so they wouldn't bump their heads on the roof of the fighting compartment, but with arms and legs like a weightlifter.

Unlike the 51-ton ISU-152, the gun on the 50-ton ISU-122 lacked a muzzle brake. Both had a front hull protected by 90mm of armour. Production of the ISU-152 and ISU-122 began in late 1943 and ended in 1945. A total of 1,665 examples of the former came out of the factory doors and 1,735 examples of the latter.

During production of the ISU-122, a call came to improve the vehicle's rate of fire by replacing the original manually-operated breechblock with a semi-automatic breechblock, the same configuration change made to the IS-2 heavy tank.

The ISU-122 self-propelled guns equipped with the new breechblock became the ISU-122S and featured a new smaller ball-shaped gun shield and a large double-baffle muzzle brake. In this case, the suffix letter 'S' is the Russian abbreviation for 'rapid fire/quick-fire'. Total production of the ISU-122S came to 675 examples by 1945.

In the Field

All three vehicles – ISU-152, ISU-122 and ISU-122S – shared the same tactical roles on the battlefield, including the destruction of German defensive positions and providing overwatch protection for T-34 and T-34/85 series medium tanks. The ISU-122 and ISU-122S found themselves preferred for engaging enemy tanks at longer ranges. The ISU-152 dealt with enemy fortifications due to its larger and more powerful HE round.

The January 1946 issue of the *Field Artillery Journal* presents an article by a Red Army officer titled 'Heavy Self-Propelled Guns in Tank Battles'. The officer noted in the following passage:

> There are two reasons why the self-propelled artillery is used in tank formations: first to free the tanks from the necessity of dueling with anti-tank guns, tanks and self-propelled guns of the enemy; and second, to enable the tanks to maneuver on the battlefield under favorable conditions. In this regard, the self-propelled artillery may be compared to a shield protecting the tank maneuver.

In a book titled *Commanding the Red Army's Sherman Tanks*, the author Dimitry Loza recalls how an ISU-152 attached to his unit dealt with a German anti-tank gun firing from a building during the battle for Vienna, Austria. The fighting for the city took place between mid-March and mid-April 1945:

The shot of the self-propelled gun's large-calibre cannon roared forth. The air itself shook. One and one-half floors of the house, together with the enemy anti-tank gun and its crew, crashed to the ground. And in our own position? With a crash, the powerful shock wave of the shot broke the thin window glass in the houses near the self-propelled gun. Heavy shards of glass poured down on the heads of our spectators. The result was lamentable: scores of wounded arms and backs and two broken collarbones. Thankfully, the tankers were wearing their headgear and the paratroopers their helmets. Their heads remained intact.

Dedicated Tank Destroyers

To supplement the SU-152, the Red Army fielded a turretless tank destroyer with the designation SU-85. It entered into production in August 1943. The four-man SU-85 was primarily based on the redundant chassis of the SU-122 and armed with an 85mm main gun. Frontal armour topped out at 50mm.

In the book *Panzer Destroyer: Memoirs of a Red Army Tank Commander* by Vasiliy Krysov appears a comparison of his newly-assigned SU-85 to his former SU-122:

The gun [85mm] had an effective direct fire range of 800–900 metres [875–984 yards] at a tank, and 600 metres [656 yards] at [anti-tank] guns, i.e. at a lower target. The rate of fire of the new gun, which used rapid-fire fired [fixed one-piece] rounds, was three times faster than that of the howitzer, which used separate loading, and the ammunition allowance increased from forty to forty-eight shells.

The 33-ton SU-85 assumed the overwatch position to support T-34-76s during offensive operations on the battlefield. Like other Red Army self-propelled guns, it lacked machine guns for self-defence.

SU-85 production ended in September 1944 as large numbers of the T-34-85 medium tank began entering service. Total production of the SU-85 amounted to 2,050 examples.

SU-100

The Red Army replacement for the SU-85 was the four-man SU-100. Like the SU-85, it was based on the chassis of the T-34 series tank but armed with a more powerful 100mm main gun. Vehicle weight came in at 35 tons due to the larger gun and increased armour protection on the front of the hull to 75mm.

The SU-100 went to elite specialized units formed in December 1944 and held under tank army control to defend against the appearance of Tiger B (Tiger II) tanks. The SU-100 first deployed in large numbers in January 1945 during the Red Army's invasion of Poland.

The right-hand-side vehicle commander's cupola was extended outward from the side of the vehicle's armoured casemate to make room for the 100mm main gun's larger breech. Due to production shortages, some early-production SU-100s left the factory armed with an 85mm main gun and became the SU-85M.

Some comments on the less than optimum design features of the SU-100 appear in a translated Red Army report dated 12 March 1945, which appears on the Tank Archives blog:

> The off-road mobility of the SU-100 is reduced compared to the T-34 tank, due to the increase in weight and shifting of the centre of mass forward due to the longer gun and thickening of the front armour. This adds additional load on the front [road] wheels. When crossing obstacles off-road, the gun can strike the ground, and then the barrel bursts when firing. The gun mount can shift during sudden turns and driving on uneven terrain. There were cases of a complete breakaway of the elevation mechanism.

Production of the SU-100 began in September 1944 and continued until 1945, with 2,355 examples completed. The vehicle would continue in production by Soviet industry until 1947. A slightly modified version of the SU-100 was licence-built in Czechoslovakia during the 1950s.

Armoured Cars

The Russian Imperial Army would employ a wide variety of armoured cars during the First World War, including some British-designed and built versions. Dissatisfaction with the British vehicles caused the Imperial Army to use home-grown armoured cars built on foreign-designed and built commercial wheeled vehicles, including British, French, Italian and American products.

The Russian Imperial Army's reliance on foreign manufacturers for the chassis of their gasoline-engine-powered armoured cars seriously limited the numbers that could be built and maintained. Eventually the Red Army would inherit most of the surviving armoured cars left over from the First World War and the Russian Civil War.

New Armoured Cars

The first post-Russian Civil War armoured car built in large numbers for the Red Army bore the designation BA-27, of which 217 came down the assembly line in 1927. The prefix 'BA' is the Russian abbreviation for 'armoured car'.

In the 1930s, the Red Army classified those armoured cars with a gun as heavy armoured cars, while those armed only with machine guns were considered light armoured cars. The primary role of armoured cars in the Red Army was reconnaissance. Some but not all Red Army armoured cars would have radios.

The BA-27 had a turret-mounted 37mm main gun and a 7.62mm machine gun. The BA-27 initially rode on the chassis of an Italian-designed but Russian-built three-axle truck with the designation AMO-F-15.

Later-production examples of the BA-27 rode on the chassis of a Ford Motors three-axle truck chassis that could better handle the vehicle's weight. It became the BA-27A, classified as a heavy armoured car.

The BA-27 series armoured cars remained in service long enough to see combat during the German invasion, with most lost in the early fighting. Some would last with the Red Army in the Far East until 1942.

D-8 and D-12 Light Armoured Cars

The Red Army decided to look into small light armoured cars armed only with machine guns in the 1930s. This led Soviet industry to come up with the two-man, two-axle D-8 and D-12. The prefix letter 'D' stood for Dyrenkov, the lead designer at the factory where these were built. Weighing in at around 2 tons, the maximum frontal armour protection on both armoured cars came to 7mm.

The D-8 and the D-12 both had two 7.62mm machine guns operated by the vehicle commander; one was in the upper front hull and the other in the upper rear hull. The Red Army experimented with having two D-8 armoured cars carried under the fuselage of the four-engine TB-3 heavy bomber, intended to land at enemy airports captured by its airborne forces. However, the experiment never led to any actual employment of the combination.

The D-12 was to be the intended replacement for the BA-27 series heavy armoured cars. Despite their poor off-road mobility and cramped interiors, the Red Army ordered both into production, with a combined total of sixty examples built. With a change of heart, the Red Army soon decided that the D-8 and D-12 were not worth keeping in service and pulled them from front-line use in 1932, restricting them only to training duties.

The Red Army, with another change of heart, decided to place both the D-8 and D-12 back into front-line service during the Russo-Finnish War and the early stages of the German invasion. Like the BA-27 series, some of the D-8 and D-12 light armoured cars would last in service with the Red Army in the Far East late in the conflict.

BA-I Light Armoured Car

The first new heavy armoured car for the Red Army proved to be the three-man BA-I armed with a turret-mounted 37mm main gun and a single 7.62mm machine gun. The suffix letter 'I' stood for the Izhorsky factory that produced 110 examples between 1932 and 1934. It rode on a Russian-built Ford Motors-designed truck chassis referred to as the GAZ-AA and weighed around 2 tons.

The replacement for the three-axle BA-I was the two-axle D-12 light armoured car, serving as the basis for the Red Army's follow-on heavy armoured cars. An upgraded version labelled the BA-IM entered service between 1939 and 1940. It rode on a newer Russian-built Ford Motors-designed truck chassis labelled the GAZ-AAA.

The two-man FAI light armoured car appeared in 1932 to replace the D-8 light armoured car based on the Ford Motors Model A two-axle chassis. Unlike the open-topped D-8, the FAI featured a turret-mounted 7.62mm machine gun. The vehicle weighed about 2 tons and had a maximum armour thickness of 8mm on the front turret. Twenty examples of the FAI were supplied to the Republican side by the Soviet Union during the Spanish Civil War.

BA-20 Light Armoured Car

The FAI light armoured car was replaced in 1936 by a very similar-looking BA-20 light armoured car. It rode on the chassis of a two-axle Russian-built GAZ-M1 car, a copy of a 1933 Ford Motors car. The approximately 2.5-ton BA-20 had a turret-mounted 7.62mm machine gun. An improved model introduced in 1938 became the BA-20M and featured a new turret design.

A modified version of the BA-20 series could ride on rails and received the designation BA-20ZhD. The suffix letters 'ZhD' are the Russian language abbreviation for 'railroad'. There were 134 examples built of the BA-2-ZhD that were configured to ride on rails.

The maximum armour thickness on the front of the BA-20 series turret was 9mm. Construction of the BA-20 series concluded in 1942 with 2,132 examples coming out of the factory.

BA-3 to BA-11 Heavy Armoured Cars

Because the BA-I three-axle heavy armoured car proved under-armoured and overweight, it remained in production for only a short time. The three-axle BA-3 armoured car that replaced it had a modified turret taken from the T-26 Model 1933 tank armed with a 45mm main gun and a 7.62mm machine gun. Three examples were supplied to the Republican side by the Soviet Union during the Spanish Civil War.

The four-man BA-3 would eventually be replaced on the assembly line by the very similar four-man BA-6 beginning in 1936. The BA-3 weighed in at about 7 tons and the BA-6 around 6 tons. Maximum armour thickness on the front turret of the BA-3 15mm and the BA-6 came in at 10mm. The Soviet Union supplied thirty-seven examples to the Republican side during the Spanish Civil War.

An improved model of the BA-6 had a more powerful engine and a smaller and lighter turret armed with a 45mm main gun and a coaxial 7.62mm machine gun and became the BA-6M. A version of the BA-6M featuring a turret-mounted

12.7mm machine gun in place of the standard 45mm main gun received the designation BA-9. However, only a few appeared due to production problems with its machine gun.

A further modernized version of the BA-6M resulted in the four-man BA-10 that entered into production in 1938. It featured frontal turret armour of 11mm thickness. As with all the other pre-Second World War armoured cars, a version of the BA-10 appeared to ride on rails. A modernized model of the BA-10 that entered into production in 1939 became the BA-10M.

The three-axle, four-man BA-11 weighed in at about 9 tons and looked very similar to the BA-10, although it proved both larger and heavier. It retained the armament configuration of the BA-10. Besides the standard gasoline-engine-powered BA-11, an experimental diesel-engine-powered version was designated the BA-11D. However, due to a shortage of diesel engines, it did not enter production.

War Intrudes

The Red Army had amassed an inventory of around 5,000 armoured cars by the time of the German invasion, with most lost in the first few months of the war in the western Soviet Union. All armoured car production ended in 1941, priority being assigned to tank production. Some of the BA-10 heavy armoured cars would last in service until 1943.

The only armoured car approved by the Red Army for production during the Second World War received the designation BA-64. The two-man vehicle had an open-topped turret armed with a 7.62mm machine gun. A small number came out of the factory in the latter part of 1942.

The BA-64 rode on the chassis of the two-axle GAZ-64 truck, based on a Ford Motors product. The prefix letters 'GAZ' are the abbreviation in Russian for the Gozky Automobile Plant, which was established with the help of the Ford Motor Company in 1932. The maximum armour thickness on the BA-64 front hull was 15mm.

An improved version of the BA-64 became the B-64A and entered into production in 1943. The roughly 3-ton vehicle retained its predecessor's armament. Approximately 11,000 examples of the GAZ-64 series came down the assembly lines by the time production concluded in 1946. The BA-64 series would also see use with Polish Army units serving alongside the Red Army during the Second World War.

Armoured Trains

The Russian Imperial Army employed many armoured trains during the First World War, both standardized and improvised designs. These armoured trains also saw use by both sides during the Russian Civil War (1917–22). With the end of the Civil War, the Red Army pulled most out of service and standardized the remaining examples.

During the interwar years, the Red Army had those armoured trains remaining in its inventory modernized and incorporated new-built armoured and armed railroad cars.

Before the German invasion, most of the Red Army's armoured trains were positioned near its western border, resulting in the majority being destroyed or captured by the German Army within the first few weeks of combat. The Germans would place some of the captured armoured trains into use for rear-area security duties.

Still seeing some usefulness for armoured trains, the Red Army had new examples built. Many incorporated tank turrets. As the war continued, however, it was clear that they had no business in front-line service. The remaining armoured trains found themselves configured for the anti-aircraft role and served behind the lines, protecting supply trains from aerial attack.

On display here is one of two prototypes constructed of the SU-14-2 armed with the 203mm Howitzer M1931 (B-4 gun). The cannon is mounted in a fixed forward-firing position with limited traverse and elevation. Soviet industry used the chassis of the T-35 heavy tank for the vehicle. The prefix letters 'SU' translate to 'self-propelled'. When originally conceived, the SU-14-2 was to be open-topped. However, with the expectation that the first two examples would see combat during the First Russo-Finnish War (1939–40), they were up-armoured, as is evident in this photograph. (*Dreamstime*)

(**Opposite, above**) As it was clear that the 54-ton SU-14-2 was impractical, the Red Army set its sights on a lighter and more affordable self-propelled gun. Two contenders appeared: the turretless SU-5-2 pictured here and the BT-7A (not shown.) The SU-5-2 had a 122mm Howitzer Model 1910/30 fitted onto the chassis of a T-26 light tank. The BT-7A came with a turret-mounted 76mm M1927 Regimental Gun. Only 33 examples of the SU-5-2 were built and fewer than 160 examples of the BT-7A. (*Dreamstime*)

(**Opposite, below**) In the late 1930s, the Red Army had industry concentrate on building tanks and placed little priority on self-propelled guns. It took until the spring of 1942 before the Red Army recognized a pressing requirement for them. What showed up was the SU-76 based on a lengthened version of the T-70 light tank chassis. Due to serious powertrain issues, only 560 SU-76s came down the assembly line before production switched to an upgraded model labelled the SU-76M, an example of which is pictured here. Both featured the 76.2mm Divisional Gun M1942 (ZiS-3). (*Dreamstime*)

(**Above**) In a photograph taken during a historical vehicle demonstration in Russia, we see a SU-76M. Open-topped, the three-man gun crew sat exposed to not only the elements but to enemy artillery and mortar airbursts. Production of the vehicle began in December 1942 and continued until 1945, with about 14,000 examples completed. With its lack of overhead armour protection and armour only 35mm thick on its front hull, the SU-76M was reserved for the infantry support role. (*Dreamstime*)

(**Above**) Based on the SU-76M's chassis, the self-propelled anti-aircraft gun labelled the ZSU-37 appeared as shown here. Production was authorized in 1944. It mounted the 37mm Automatic Air Defence Gun M1939 (61-K). Unlike the SU-76M with its fixed open-topped casemate, the ZSU-37 featured a 360-degree open-topped traversable turret. Hampered by a slow turret traverse speed which made it difficult for the crew to track and engage fast low-flying aircraft, only a few hundred were produced. (*Vladimir Yakubov*)

(**Opposite, above**) Closely following authorization for the SU-76/SU-76M, the Red Army authorized development of a medium self-propelled gun based on the T-34 chassis and armed with the 122mm Howitzer M1938 (M-30). The cannon was fitted into an armoured casemate as pictured here, with limited traverse and elevation. The final product seen here received the label SU-122, with production beginning in December 1942. (*Dreamstime*)

(**Opposite, below**) A German soldier examines a knocked-out SU-122. The vehicle was 22ft in length, had a width of about 11ft and was 8ft tall. The five-man crew was protected by frontal armour 45mm thick. It had limited success in combat due to poor armour penetration by its tank-killing rounds. Preferring more effective self-propelled guns, the Red Army cancelled production in mid-1943 after 1,148 examples had been completed. (*Author's collection*)

(**Above**) A more effective self-propelled gun than the SU-122 was the SU-152 pictured here. Instead of the T-34 chassis, industry used the KV-1S chassis. The cannon fitted into the armoured casemate was a muzzle-brake-equipped 152mm Howitzer Gun M1937 (ML-20). The vehicle had a five-man crew that was protected by a maximum frontal armour thickness of 60mm. Production began in February 1943, with the first examples entering front-line service in May 1943. Production of the SU-152 concluded by the end of 1943, with 704 examples built. (*Dreamstime*)

(**Opposite**) A German Army NCO (non-commissioned officer) poses for the photographer holding a projectile from the SU-152 behind him. The vehicle had authorized storage for twenty of the 152mm separately-loaded rounds. Due to the rounds' size and weight, the vehicle's rate of fire was two rounds per minute. Although the SU-152 is best-known for its role as a tank destroyer, its original intended job was as an assault gun dealing with enemy defensive fortifications. (*Author's collection*)

(**Above**) Inside a Soviet factory we see what looks like the rebuilding of SU-152s rather than an assembly line producing new examples. The blast effect generated by the cannon's HE rounds led to them being able to punch through the thick vertical frontal armour of Tiger tanks and the well-sloped frontal armour of Panther tanks. It proved less successful in dealing with the thick, strong armour of the Ferdinand/Elefant tank destroyers that were encountered during the Battle of Kursk in the summer of 1943. (*Author's collection*)

(**Opposite, above**) With production of the KV-1S heavy tank coming to an end in April 1943, the Red Army saw the chassis of the new IS-2 heavy tank as the logical replacement for its next generation of self-propelled guns. That would include one version armed with the same 152mm Howitzer Gun M1937 (ML-20) that armed the SU-152 and another armed with the 122mm Gun M1931/37 (A-19). Pictured here is an example of the former, assigned the designation ISU-152. (*Dreamstime*)

(**Opposite, below**) On display at the Finnish Army tank museum is an ISU-152, which looked much like the SU-152 from a distance. The ISU-152 and ISU-122 have a taller, less-sloped armoured casemate than their predecessor. Compared to the 60mm-thick frontal armour on the SU-152, the ISU-152 and ISU-122 had a maximum frontal armour thickness of 90mm. Production of both vehicles began in late 1943 and ended in 1945. Production totalled 1,665 examples of the former and 1,735 of the latter. (*Dreamstime*)

(**Above**) Seen here taking part in a parade are two examples of the ISU-122. Due to the vehicles' manually-operated breech mechanism the rate of fire was limited to about one round per minute. By arming the ISU-122 with a new version of the A-19 gun with a semi-automatic breechblock, the rate of fire was increased to almost four rounds per minute with a well-trained crew. Vehicles so fitted appeared with a double-baffle muzzle brake and were assigned the designation of ISU-122S. Their gun shield was smaller than that on the ISU-122. (*Author's collection*)

(**Opposite, above**) As the cannons on the SU-152, ISU-152 and ISU-122 were general-purpose weapons rather than purpose-built anti-tank guns, the Red Army studied fielding a heavier anti-tank self-propelled gun based on the T-34 chassis to counter the increasingly thick armour on German tanks. The result was the SU-85 pictured here, armed with a cannon based on the Air Defence Gun M1938 (52-K). Production began in August 1943 and ended in 1944 when the T-34-85 began showing up in large numbers. (*Dreamstime*)

(**Below**) The Red Army replacement for the SU-85 was the SU-100 pictured here. From a distance, the difference between the two dedicated tank destroyers is challenging to discern. When viewed more closely, it is evident that the gun barrel on the SU-100 is longer and thicker. To accommodate the 100mm gun's larger breech the vehicle commander's cupola was displaced to the right, partially outside the armoured casemate as shown in this image. Whereas the SU-85 glacis was 45mm thick, that on the SU-100 came to 75mm. (*Dreamstime*)

(**Opposite, above**) The armoured casemate roof details of a SU-100. The vehicle commander's cupola in the foreground is the same as that on the T-34-85. Directly behind the
cupola are two mushroom-shaped armoured domes that protect the electrically-powered
ventilation fans beneath them. Visible behind the cupola is the open loader's single-piece
overhead hatch. In front of that hatch is the open two-piece hatch for the gunner which,
like the commander's overhead hatch, has a 360-degree traversable periscope. (*Dreamstime*)

(**Opposite, below**) The Russian Imperial Army did not field any tanks during the First
World War. However, it did acquire some foreign armoured cars. The most numerous
proved to be a British-designed and built armoured car designed and built by the Austin
Motor Company. It had two one-man machine-gun-armed turrets. The vehicle pictured
here is a Russian copy of the British vehicle. Examples of foreign armoured cars and
improvised Russian-built versions lasted long enough to be taken into service by the Red
Army. (*Dreamstime*)

(**Above**) One of the first armoured cars built for the Red Army, the turretless D-8,
appeared in 1931 and was based on a commercial Ford Motor car chassis built under
licence in the Soviet Union. The vehicle's superstructure featured several armoured gun
ports for firing onboard machine guns. The two men of the D-8's crew sat back-to-back,
so the crewman in the rear seat could fire at potential enemy personnel or vehicles behind
or following the D-8. (*Dreamstime*)

(**Opposite, above**) The D-8 and an open-topped version labelled the D-12 found themselves being replaced starting in 1931 by a machine-gun-armed turreted armoured car labelled the FAI. The most numerous prewar armoured cars in prewar service were the three-man BA-20s fielded in 1936 and an improved version, the BA-20M, in 1938. Several are seen here on parade. They provided an enhanced degree of off-road mobility compared to their predecessors. (*Author's collection*)

(**Opposite, below**) The non-sloping side walls of the machine-gun-armed turret on this armoured car identify it as a BA-20. The turret on the BA-20M had slightly sloping side armour plates. This particular example of the BA-20 has all-steel wheels that allow it to ride on railroad tracks. This was a common arrangement implemented by many armies pre-Second World War when suitable roads were lacking and railroads were a prime target for sabotage. (*Dreamstime*)

(**Above**) The Red Army categorized its armoured cars by their armament. Those armed only with machine guns were light armoured cars, and those with cannons were either medium or heavy armoured cars. An example of the latter, designated the BA-3, is pictured here. It is fitted with a turret from a mid-production T-26 light tank. There were other prewar two-axle and three-axle armoured cars with various cannon-armed turrets. (*Dreamstime*)

(**Opposite, above**) The Red Army's prewar interest in amphibious light tanks in the early 1930s sparked interest in an amphibious car. The single prototype was labelled the BAD-2, but after testing it never went anywhere. In 1935 work began on another amphibious armoured car, the PB-4 pictured here and fitted with a modified T-26 light tank turret. Testing showed that the PB-4 was too heavy and underpowered, leading to its cancellation. (*Dreamstime*)

(**Above**) In the early days of the German invasion, things looked bleak and heavy losses of men and equipment rattled everybody in the Soviet Union from the top downwards. Some factories took it upon themselves to build an array of improvised armoured vehicles with whatever was on hand. An example of that effort is seen here with a reproduction vehicle, no doubt based on some pictorial evidence. Industry also modified commercial farm tractors into ad-hoc tanks. (*Dreamstime*)

(**Opposite, below**) Before the German invasion, the Red Army had amassed an inventory of almost 5,000 armoured cars. However, once the Germans attacked, all armoured car production was halted; industry was tasked to build only tanks. Some of the prewar armoured cars would last in ever-decreasing numbers until the end of the war. The sole armoured wheeled vehicle authorized by the Red Army for production during the Second World War was the two-man BA-64 seen here. Open-topped, the vehicle had only a 7.62mm machine gun for armament. (*Dreamstime*)

(**Above**) Production of the BA-64 and an improved version, the BA-64B, began in 1942. They entered service in large numbers by early 1943. The vehicles seen here rode on the 4 × 4 chassis of either GAZ-64 or GAZ-67 light trucks. The hull design of the BA-64 series found itself loosely based on the multi-faceted design of the German 4 × 4 Sd.Kfz.221 armoured cars. Sources suggest that about 9,000 examples of the BA-64 series armoured cars were built by 1946. (*Author's collection*)

(**Opposite, above**) Seen here is a Red Army T-20 Armoured Tractor Komsomolyets. It had an armoured cab for its two-man crew and was armed with a 7.62mm machine gun. It served as a prime mover for light artillery pieces and the PM-38 120mm mortar. It also provided seating for six men. For protection from the elements, the passengers had a canvas cover which is not seen in this image. However, the metal framework to support it is shown. About 11,000 examples of the prime mover came off the factory floor between 1937 and 1941. (*SA-Kuva*)

(**Opposite, below**) Such was the demand for self-propelled guns in early 1943 that the Red Army gave industry its approval to manufacture self-propelled guns based on the captured chassis of Panzer III medium tanks and StuG. III assault guns. The first iteration seen here was the SG-122 armed with the 122mm Howitzer M1938 (M-30) fitted into an armoured casemate. The initial order called for 120 examples. However, the resulting product proved disappointing and only twenty-one of them appeared before its cancellation. (*Dreamstime*)

(**Above**) Following the SG-122, another attempt was made by Soviet industry to convert the chassis of captured Panzer III medium tanks and StuG. III assault guns into self-propelled guns. Armament was to be a 76mm gun based on the F-34 gun that armed the T-34. This strange combination with an example pictured here became the SU-76i. About 200 examples entered front-line service. The suffix letter denoted that the vehicle's chassis came from a foreign design. (*Dreamstime*)

(**Opposite, above**) The Imperial Russian Army had fielded many armoured trains before and during the First World War. A number of these would see service during the Russian Civil War (1917–22). The Red Army continued to believe in the value of armoured trains throughout the Second World War. An example is seen here with one car of a steam-engine-powered armoured train labelled the BP-43. It features an armoured enclosure topped off with a turret of a T-34. A typical BP-43 would pull four of these weapon-armed flatcars. (*Dreamstime*)

(**Opposite, below**) The self-propelled armoured railcar pictured here is armed with the 45mm gun-armed turret from a T-26 light tank. Only five examples were built and received the designation of the BDT, with four going on to see service with the Red Army in the Far East. The remaining example would see combat with the Red Army during the First Russo-Finnish War (1939–40) and later on the Leningrad Front. It was badly damaged in an aerial attack in August 1941 but was rebuilt and placed back into service. (*Author's collection*)

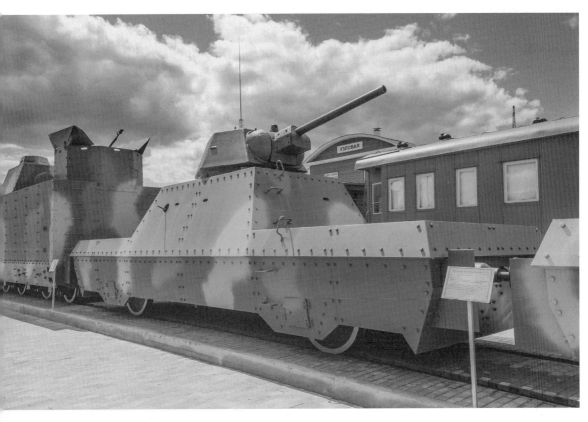

Between 1936 and 1937 Soviet industry built two examples of a self-propelled armoured railcar labelled the MBV, with the surviving example pictured here. The MBV's gasoline engine came from the T-28 medium tank. Armament was three L-11 76.2mm gun-armed turrets. The MBV pictured had its original 76.2mm L-11 guns replaced by longer-barrelled F-34 guns from the T-34. Besides the 76.2mm guns, the MBV came with four machine guns. Eventually a fifth machine gun went onto its roof for anti-aircraft protection. (*Dreamstime*)

Chapter Seven

Imported Weapons

The United States began supporting the Soviet Union with a wide variety of military and non-military equipment starting in November 1941. Among these items was an assortment of tanks and armoured fighting vehicles (AFVs).

Both the military and non-military goods were provided to the Soviet Union under a programme generally referred to as 'Lend-Lease'. Its official title, 'An Act to Promote the United States Defense', was approved by the American Congress in March 1941. The purpose was to help keep the Soviet Union in the war.

The Contribution

The United States, under Lend-Lease, supplied the Soviet Union with approximately 7,000 tanks and 5,000 AFVs during the Second World War. Included were armoured scout cars and armoured half-tracks; all would arrive with their standard US Army authorization of machine guns and small arms. Also supplied to the Soviet Union by the United States were towed anti-aircraft guns and associated fire-control equipment.

In the big picture of Lend-Lease, the Red Army believed that the hundreds of thousands of American trucks supplied were far more critical to their war effort. The reason was that Soviet industry could devote itself to building more tanks rather than trucks for the Red Army.

Light Tanks

Under Lend-Lease 1,676 American M3 light tanks went off by ship to the Soviet Union between 1942 and 1943. Of that number, 340 were the M3A1 variant. Some 443 of the approximately 14-ton American light tanks never arrived as the cargo ships transporting them were sunk in the Atlantic and Arctic Oceans by German attacks.

In Red Army service, the M3/M3A1 became the M3L, with the suffix letter 'L' representing the Russian language abbreviation for the word 'light'. The Red Army thought highly of the penetrative abilities of the tank's 37mm AP ammunition but disliked the vehicle's height as it made them a larger target on the battlefield.

Five examples of the 37mm main gun-armed M5 light tank and two 75mm main gun-armed M24 light tanks eventually reached the Soviet Union under Lend-Lease. After evaluation, the Red Army expressed no interest in acquiring additional examples of either. The United States would also supply a single M26 Pershing heavy tank.

M3 Medium Tank

The first medium tanks allocated to the Soviet Union under Lend-Lease in 1942 were 1,386 gasoline-engine-powered M3s. Of that number, 410 failed to arrive as German naval attacks sank the merchant ships transporting them.

The Red Army assigned the 30-ton M3 medium tank the designation 'M3S'. Red Army tankers appreciated the reliability of the M3 medium tank compared to the poor reliability of early-production T-34 series tanks. However, they found fault with the American vehicle's height and thinner armour. The M3 medium tank had a height of 10ft 3in, whereas the T-34-76 came in at 7ft 10in. The maximum armour thickness on the M3 medium tank was 50mm.

Especially bothersome for Red Army tankers was the American tanks' dependence on gasoline rather than the less volatile diesel fuel standard in most Soviet tanks. Gasoline-engine-powered tanks were more prone to burning when penetrated by enemy AP projectiles. That concern reached the highest levels of Soviet leadership, as seen referenced in an 18 July 1942 letter from Joseph Stalin to American President Franklin D. Roosevelt: 'US tanks catch fire very easily when hit from behind or from the side.'

M4 Medium Tanks

As the US upgraded from the M3 medium tank to the M4 series, the Soviet Union received 1,780 examples of the approximately 30-ton diesel-engine-powered M4A2 medium tank armed with a 75mm main gun. The bulk of M4A2 medium tanks arrived in the Soviet Union in 1944. Those that arrived in 1942 had some problems, as seen in the following extract from the Sherman Minutia website:

> The Tank Section of the American Supply Mission to the USSR was 'charged with making the Lend-Lease tank program effective'. However, its efforts were severely limited since, as of February 1943, it consisted of only one officer, Colonel Edward Grey, and three civilian technicians. A training school was established at the Gorky Reception Center for Foreign Vehicles, but 'lack of adequate assistance ... in many cases has resulted in premature failure of the equipment in Red Army hands ... these difficulties have resulted in a lack of appreciation of the value of American tank equipment, and doubt in the minds of officials of the Soviet Government as to the ability of the United States to make the tank section of the Lend-Lease program effective.'

The more refined M4A2s delivered in 1944 suffered from fewer reliability issues than the examples delivered earlier. The Red Army impressions of these later examples of the M4A2 with the 75mm main gun ran the gamut from 'we would rather have more trucks or armoured half-tracks' to 'the tank was not that bad'. One Red Army report noted 'Compared to the T-34, the M4A2 is more easily controllable, more resilient during long marches, as the engines do not require frequent adjustment. In battle, these tanks work well.'

Within the book *T-34 in Action: Soviet Tank Troops in World War II* is a comment made by a former Red Army tanker on his wartime impression of the M4A2: 'I had a look at an American M4A2 Sherman. My God! It was like a hotel inside! It was all lined in leather so that you didn't smash your head. There was a medical kit with condoms and sulfide – they had everything!'

In addition to the 75mm gun-armed M4A2, the Soviet Union received 2,073 examples of the improved diesel-engine-powered M4A2 armed with a 76mm main gun. On their data plates it read Tank, Medium, M4A2 76mm Gun, Wet. The suffix word 'Wet' meant that most of its main gun rounds were stored in liquid-filled containers in the tank's hull below the fighting compartment to reduce the risk of ammunition-fuelled fires. These began arriving in the Soviet Union in late 1944.

American factories built 2,915 examples of the M4A2 armed with the 76mm main gun and with the 'Wet' stowage configuration. Most of those shipped to the Soviet Union rode on the original Vertical Volute Suspension System (VVSS). Those delivered near the end of the war featured the improved Horizontal Volute Spring Suspension (HVSS) system. None of the HVSS-equipped M4A2s would see combat during the Second World War with the Red Army.

Red Army tankers nicknamed their M4 series tanks armed with the 75mm main gun the 'Emcha' from the first letter and number of its alpha-numeric designation. Those armed with the larger main gun became known by some as the 'Emcha-76'.

Russian weather proved a problem for American tanks. Their smooth rubber block trackpads failed to provide traction on ice-covered surfaces. Sometimes this resulted in tanks overturning. In the book *Commanding the Red Army's Sherman Tanks*, former Red Army tanker Colonel Dmitriy Loza describes the problem:

> Many tank commanders and driver-mechanics instinctively felt that the first cause of the disaster was the rubber-shoed track. They began to modify it by installing makeshift cleats. They twisted barbed wire on the outside edges of the track and installed bolts in the openings of the track blocks. The results were immediate ... Brigade and battalion maintenance units began urgently to install cleats on the tracks (at any moment, an order might come down to road march to another position). In two hours, the Shermans had been 'reshoed'.

Loza listed other reasons for the American tanks' instability when travelling over ice-covered surfaces. These included their height, relatively narrow width and weight distribution, resulting in a high centre of gravity. In comparison, Loza mentioned that the much lower height and broader width of the T-34 series meant that they rarely turned over.

Of the 3,459 examples of the M4A2 series (both those armed with the 75mm and 76mm main guns) placed on merchant ships for transport to the Soviet Union, about 400 never arrived as German naval attacks sank the vessels transporting them. Later-production M4A2 tanks arriving in the Soviet Union had all-steel tracks featuring built-in grousers.

The United States also supplied the Soviet Union with two examples of the M4A4 medium tank in May 1943. The complexity and maintenance requirements of its five-engine, thirty-cylinder gasoline-powered multibank engine arrangement and its high fuel consumption compared to the M4A2 left the Red Army unimpressed.

Scout Cars and Half-Tracks

The most numerous American AFV acquired by the Red Army through Lend-Lease proved to be the 3,340 examples of the two-axle M3A1 scout car, with only six lost at sea. The open-topped machine gun-armed vehicle primarily served in the reconnaissance role with the Red Army, with some acting as prime movers towing anti-tank guns.

Besides the M3A1 scout car, the Red Army received around 1,000 machine gun-armed open-topped examples of various armoured half-tracks. The majority of these approximately 10-ton vehicles came from the International Harvester Corporation. Due to their limited numbers, their primary role with the Red Army was that of command post vehicles or as a prime mover for anti-tank guns.

Anti-Aircraft Half-Tracks

A specialized variant of the armoured half-track series that the Red Army received under Lend-Lease bore the label M17 Multiple Gun Motor Carriage (MGMC). Armament consisted of four .50-calibre air-cooled Browning machine guns mounted on an electrically-powered Maxson one-man armoured turret in the vehicle's rear cargo bay. The entire production run of 1,000 examples of the M17 went to the Soviet Union.

The United States also shipped to the Soviet Union under Lend-Lease 100 examples of the M15 MGMC armed with a single 37mm automatic cannon and two .50-calibre Browning air-cooled machine guns in a combination mount. Protection for the gun crew came from a three-sided open-topped gun shield.

Tank Destroyers

Among the various armoured half-tracks provided to the Red Army under Lend-Lease was the American-designated T48 GMC (Gun Motor Carriage). It had a forward-firing 6-pounder (57mm) main gun with limited traverse and elevation. Out of a production run of 962 examples, 650 went to the Red Army and received the designation SU-57.

In addition the Red Army received fifty-two examples of the M10 3in GMC. As the M10 rode on the modified chassis of an M4A2 medium tank, it received power from two diesel engines. The Red Army classified the vehicle as a self-propelled gun (SU). Besides the M10, a handful of M18 GMCs also arrived in the Soviet Union via Lend-Lease. However, the Red Army was unimpressed with the tank destroyer and chose not to request any additional examples.

British-Supplied Armour

The Soviet Union, under a mutual aid agreement from the British government, received 5,218 British-designed tanks during the Second World War. Not all would survive the journey to the Soviet Union due to German attacks on the merchant ships transporting the vehicles.

Those British government-supplied tanks that did arrive in the Soviet Union in late 1941 made up to 40 per cent of the Red Army tank strength defending Moscow in December 1941.

Of the four different types of tanks provided to the Soviet Union by the British government, their preferred model was the diesel-engine-powered Valentine series. The British government authorized the transfer of 3,378 examples, with 235 of those lost at sea. Even before the first Valentine tanks were shipped off to the Soviet Union, the British Army had declared the Valentine tank obsolete.

In the book titled *T-34 Tanks in Action: Soviet Tank Troops in WWII*, a former Red Army tanker commented on the Valentine: 'It was a very successful tank, low to the ground, with a powerful gun and a quiet engine.'

Of the Valentine tanks shipped to the Soviet Union, 1,388 were licence-built Canadian examples. These proved more popular with the Red Army as they featured an American-designed and built diesel engine superior to its British-designed and built counterpart. With a steady supply of Valentine tanks, Soviet industry ended light tank production in 1943.

In the Red Army classification system, the three-man Valentine fell within the category of a light tank. Maximum frontal armour thickness on the tank came to 60mm. The 17-ton Valentine version initially provided to the Soviet Union had a 2-pounder (40mm) main gun.

Red Army displeasure with the 2-pounder (40mm) led to the British government providing it with 927 examples of the Valentine that featured a 6-pounder (57mm) main gun. Due to the size of the 6-pounder breech, those so armed lacked a coaxial 7.92mm machine gun. The standard coaxial machine gun for British-built tanks was the 'Besa', a British version of a Czech-designed machine gun.

Matilda II Tank

The Red Army acquired 918 examples of the 28-ton Matilda II out of the 1,084 shipped by the British government. Design work on the tank began in 1936, with the first production examples entering British Army service in 1939. Maximum frontal armour protection was 78mm, superior to that of the T-34 and equal to that on the early-production KV-1.

The Matilda II featured a 2-pounder main gun and a coaxial 7.92mm machine gun. The Red Army disliked the 2-pounder gun as it had on the Valentine because it had no high-explosive (HE) round. Therefore, it proved difficult for the tank crews to engage towed anti-tank gun crews.

To address the issue of the 2-pounder gun on the Matilda, Soviet industry received orders to fit a 76.2mm gun into the tank. However, only 47 of the 120 ordered made it off the production line before the Red Army lost interest in the project. Responding to the Red Army's disappointment with the Matilda II's main gun, the British government eventually sent 156 examples of an up-gunned version armed with a 3in howitzer, identified by the suffix letters 'CS' for close support.

The Red Army also disliked the Matilda due to its maximum speed of only 16mph. As the British Army classified the Matilda as an infantry support tank, high speed was an unnecessary design attribute.

Because the Matilda performed poorly in the climatic conditions of a Soviet winter, the Red Army informed the British official overseeing military deliveries in December 1941 that they wanted no more examples of the tank shipped to them. However, as the British had nothing else to send, they continued shipping Matilda tanks to the Soviet Union through to 1942.

In the book titled *T-34 Tanks in Action: Soviet Tank Troops in WWII*, a former Red Army tanker commented on the design flaws he perceived with the Matilda II: 'But the Matilda … It was clumsy, had poor manoeuvring capabilities. Its two weak 90hp Leyland engines could barely make it go 25kph [16mph] on a road, and on an unpaved road even less!'

Churchill Tank

In the summer of 1942 the British government shipped to the Soviet Union the first 30 Churchill tanks out of an eventual total of 258 examples. Of the first thirty shipped, twenty went down with the merchant ships carrying them.

The five-man Churchill tanks that entered Red Army service came armed with a 6-pounder (57mm) main gun and three 7.92mm machine guns. The approximately 43-ton tank had a maximum frontal armour protection level of 102mm. In Red Army service the gasoline-engine-powered tank fell into the heavy tank category. Its top speed on level roads was 15mph.

The British government had been reluctant to provide the Churchill to the Soviet Union due to its many early-production design issues, but had nothing else to send. During testing of one of the Churchills, the Red Army confirmed its unsuitability for field use. Despite this, the Red Army put them on the front lines, with a few lasting in service until 1944.

The Universal Carrier

The only British-designed AFV supplied to the Soviet Union was the full-track Universal Carrier and a smaller number of variants. A total of 1,212 came from British factories, with another 1,348 from Canada. The open-topped vehicles weighed approximately 4 tons and had maximum armour protection of 10mm. Powered by gasoline engines, their top speed on level roads was 30mph.

The Universal Carrier had entered British Army service in 1940, derived from the 1920s-era Carden Loyd Machine Gun Carrier. The Universal Carrier's armament typically consisted of a single 7.7mm Bren machine gun, a British copy of a Czech-designed light machine gun.

Many of the Universal Carriers shipped to the Soviet Union also came armed with the bolt-action .55 Boys Anti-Tank Rifle. When introduced into service with the British Army in the late 1930s, it stood a chance of penetrating existing light tank armour. By the 1940s, it was only truly effective against very thinly-armoured vehicles such as armoured cars or armoured half-tracks. In Red Army service, the Universal Carriers served as reconnaissance vehicles or as general-purpose utility vehicles.

Odds and Ends

In 1942 the British government delivered to the Soviet Union twenty examples of the Tetrarch gasoline-engine-powered light tank. The three-man tank weighed approximately 8 tons and had a 2-pounder (40mm) main gun and a coaxial 7.92mm machine gun.

Despite the small number of Tetrarch tanks supplied and the Red Army's dislike of the 2-pounder main gun, they placed them into front-line service as is evident from some officially released wartime photographs.

The British government also shipped to the Soviet Union three examples of a flame-thrower-equipped version of the Churchill known as the Crocodile and three examples of a mine-clearing vehicle based on the American M4 medium tank series referred to as the Crab.

Shipped to the Soviet Union in 1944 were six Cromwell tanks armed with a 75mm main gun, the British intention being to interest the Red Army in replacing its Valentines with the more modern Cromwell. However, the Red Army proved uninterested in the Cromwell. It continued to request more Valentines, much to the disbelief of the British officials overseeing the military aid programme who saw the latter as obsolete by that point in the war.

Besides the tanks and the Universal Carrier, the British government also supplied the Soviet Union with 636 examples of the 2-pounder towed anti-tank gun as well as 96 examples of the 6-pounder towed anti-tank gun. The latter was the same weapon mounted on the SU-57. In theory the 6-pounder could penetrate 74mm of armour sloped at 30 degrees from a distance of 1,000 yards.

To supplement the towed anti-tank guns, the British government sent 1,000 examples of the man-portable Projector, Infantry, Anti-Tank (PIAT) gun. The 32lb weapon fired a shaped-charge warhead that had an effective direct-fire range of 115 yards. It had entered British Army service in late 1942 and, when carried by a brave and resolute soldier, proved itself capable of destroying the most thickly armoured tanks at close range.

(**Above**) The armoured vehicles supplied to the Red Army under Lend-Lease included the US M3 light tank and slightly improved M3A1 light tanks, with an example of the latter pictured here. The M3 had a vehicle commander's cupola, while the M3A1 did not. Of the 1,676 M3 series light tanks shipped to the Soviet Union, 1,336 were the M3 variant and the other 340 units were the M3A1 version. Both vehicles were powered by gasoline engines and manned by a crew of four. (*Dreamstime*)

(**Opposite, above**) In the collection of a Russian museum is this M3A1 light tank. This example has a welded hull and turret instead of the riveted hull and turret of early-production M3 series tanks. Both versions had a cast homogenous armour (CHA) gun shield. Despite American industry building a diesel-engine-powered M3 series tank, none went to the Soviet Union under Lend-Lease, despite the Red Army's preference for diesel-engine-powered tanks. (*Dreamstime*)

(**Opposite, below**) The first American medium tank provided to the Soviet Union under Lend-Lease was the 31-ton M3 pictured here. A total of 1,386 examples of the gasoline-engine-powered vehicle were shipped to the Soviet Union, but not all arrived due to the German attacks on convoys to Murmansk. However, the Red Army was not thrilled with the awkward arrangement of its weapons or its height of about 10ft. The hull of the M3 medium tank pictured is riveted rolled homogenous armour (RHA) and the turret is CHA. (*Dreamstime*)

(**Above**) The next American medium tank received under Lend-Lease by the Red Army was the first-generation twin diesel-engine-powered M4A2 armed with a 75mm main gun. American industry built 8,053 examples of the tank between April 1942 and May 1944, with almost all going to Lend-Lease. The Red Army received about 2,000 examples. They found the M4A2 more reliable than their T-34, but found it hampered by its poor armour arrangement and its height. (*Dreamstime*)

(**Opposite, above**) Following first-generation M4A2 tanks armed with a 75mm main gun were 2,007 examples of the second-generation M4A2 armed with a 76mm main gun and 'Wet' ammunition storage. These, however, still rode on the same Vertical Volute Suspension System (VVSS) as the first-generation M4A2, resulting in higher ground pressure and reduced mobility. An issue with all Lend-Lease tanks was an inconsistent supply of spare parts and ammunition. (*Dreamstime*)

(**Opposite, below**) The final version of the M4A2 series provided to the Soviet Union under Lend-Lease was a second-generation version. Armed with the same 76mm main gun and Wet ammunition, these now rode on the wider and much improved Horizontal Volute Spring Suspension (HVSS) system. However, these vehicles arrived too late to see combat before the war's end. (*Dreamstime*)

(**Opposite, above**) Besides first-generation M4A2s, the United States also provided five examples of the first-generation M4A4 medium tank for their consideration. One of the five is pictured here in a Russian military museum. The M4A4 was powered by the Chrysler Multi-Bank engine, which consisted of five inline gasoline engines coupled to a common driveshaft. The Red Army had no interest in that version and none were requested. (*Dreamstime*)

(**Opposite, below**) Another American tank provided to the Soviet Union by way of Lend-Lease for their consideration consisted of five examples of the M5 light tank, one of which appears here in a Russian military museum. Like its predecessors in the M3 series, the M5 and the improved M5A1 received power from gasoline engines. Rather than the aircraft-based gasoline radial engines of the M3 and M3A1, the M5 tank was powered by two Cadillac automobile engines coupled to a common driveshaft via an automatic hydraulic transmission. (*Dreamstime*)

(**Above**) Two examples of the US M24 light tank also went to the Soviet Union under Lend-Lease. Powered by the same twin gasoline-powered automobile engine arrangement of the M5 series, the M24 tank pictured here had a 75mm main gun. That gun was adapted from one developed for specially-configured American B-25 medium bombers designed to attack enemy shipping in the Pacific Theatre of Operation. (*Pierre-Olivier Buan*)

(**Above**) Among the wheeled armoured fighting vehicles provided to the Soviet Union was the US M3A1 Scout Car. An example of the roughly 4-ton vehicle is pictured here at an historical event in Russia. The American military thought little of the gasoline-engine-powered M3A1 Scout Car and had almost all 11,000 examples built allocated to Lend-Lease. The Red Army received about 3,000. What they thought of the vehicle was unimportant as all quickly entered service. (*Dreamstime*)

(**Opposite, above**) All the various tanks and other armoured fighting vehicles supplied to the Soviet Union by way of Lend-Lease were equipped with crew weapons such as hand grenades and submachine guns. Pictured here is a mid-production US M1928A1. It differed from the earlier M1921 as it had a small knob-like cocking handle on the top of its receiver and a compensator at the muzzle end of the barrel. (*Dreamstime*)

(**Opposite, below**) Red Army soldiers are posing for the photographer with one of two M1919A4 .30 calibre machine guns that typically armed the M3A1 Scout Car. These guns were mounted on a 'skate rail' that circled most of the fighting compartment, allowing the crew to slide them to a point where they could bear on a target. Typically the M3A1 Scout Car also had a single .50 calibre (12.7mm) M2 Heavy Barrel (HB) air-cooled machine gun mounted on a pedestal. (*Author's collection*)

(**Above**) An early wartime picture of US Army soldiers taking their half-tracks out for a spin. The Red Army received about 1,200 examples of American-built half-tracks during the Second World War. These included the Half-Track Car M2, the Half-Track Car M9A1 and the Half-Track Personnel Carrier M5. The M9A1 and M5 were built by the American firm of International Harvester exclusively for Lend-Lease. (*PICRYL*)

(**Opposite, above**) A half-track-based variant acquired by the Red Army was the US 57mm Gun Motor Carriage (GMC) T48. The chassis is that of a modified Half-Track Personnel Carrier M3. Originally intended for the British Army, the vehicle was armed with an American-built version of what the British Army referred to as a 6-pounder. However, of the 962 examples manufactured, the British Army only took thirty of them in the end. The remaining 650 were shipped to the Soviet Union under Lend-Lease instead. (*Dreamstime*)

(**Opposite, below**) The American government shipped to the Soviet Union two different types of anti-aircraft-armed half-tracks. The example pictured here is the Half-Track Combination Gun Motor Carriage (CGMC) M15A1. Armament consisted of a single 37mm automatic cannon and two .50 calibre (12.7mm) M2 Heavy Barrel (HB) air-cooled machine guns. The other anti-aircraft half-track provided (but not pictured) was the Half-Track Multiple Gun Motor Carriage (MGMC) M17, built on the M5A1 and armed with four .50 calibre (12.7mm) machine guns. (*Author's collection*)

(**Above**) For technical evaluation, the Red Army received five examples of the US M18 76mm Gun Motor Carriage (GMC.) It had an open-topped CHA turret armed with a 76mm main gun and an RHA welded hull. The tank destroyer was the first American military tracked vehicle to ride on a torsion bar suspension system. Power came from an air-cooled radial aircraft engine that provided a maximum speed on level roads of 60mph, making it the fastest combat vehicle fielded during the Second World War. (*Richard Eshleman*)

(**Opposite, above**) Other American open-topped tank destroyers shipped off to the Soviet Union were fifty-two of the 3in GMC M10, with a restored example shown here. The vehicle rode on the modified chassis of the diesel-engine-powered first-generation M4A2 medium tank. Another version consisted of the modified chassis of the gasoline-engine-powered first-generation M4A3 medium tank and received the designation M10A1. (*Pierre-Olivier Buan*)

(**Opposite, below**) The British government supplied the Soviet Union with different types of tanks during the Second World War. Due to its reliability, the Red Army's favourite was the Infantry Tank Mark III, better known as the Valentine. Most featured a 2-pounder (40mm) main gun as on the example pictured here. A later-production version sent to the Soviet Union came with a 6-pounder (57mm) gun. Of the roughly 8,000 Valentines built, 3,872 went off to the Red Army. Almost half the Valentine tanks provided to the Soviet Union were Canadian-built. (*Dreamstime*)

(**Above**) Another tank type sent to the Soviet Union as military aid by the British government included different models of the infantry tank known as the 'Matilda II'. The Red Army disliked its 2-pounder (40mm) main gun as it did not have an HE round. Another problem encountered by the Red Army was the tank's enclosed armoured suspension system that quickly became crammed with snow, ice and mud, hindering its mobility. In combat, slow or immobile tanks became easy targets. In total, the Red Army received approximately 2,000 Matilda tanks. (*Dreamstime*)

(**Opposite, above**) German soldiers are seen here inspecting a knocked-out Red Army Matilda II. Due to the tank's small turret, British industry could not up-arm it with the 6-pounder (57mm) main gun that they'd used for late-production Valentine infantry tanks. Power for the Matilda II came from two diesel engines. Red Army tankers operating the tank appreciated the protection afforded by its 78mm-thick frontal armour, but disliked its maximum road speed of only 16mph. (*Dreamstime*)

(**Opposite, below**) Pictured here is an Infantry Tank Mk VI referred to as a 'Churchill' and armed with a 75mm main gun. The Red Army received 250 examples of the tank in three different variants: the Mk II armed with a 2-pounder (40mm) main gun, and the Mk III and Mk IV both armed with the 6-pounder (57mm) main gun. The tank's thick armour was much appreciated by Red Army tankers. However, like the Matilda tanks, the Churchill tanks' armoured enclosed suspension system would quickly become clogged with mud, snow and ice, leading to mobility problems. (*PICRYL*)

(**Above**) The British government provided the Red Army with six examples of the Cruiser Tank referred to as the 'Cromwell' in August 1944. Their armament included a British-designed and built 75mm gun and two 7.92mm machine guns. The Red Army tested the Cromwell, an example of which is pictured here, against the American Lend-Lease first- and second-generation M4A2 medium tanks. It found the Cromwell wanting in every respect except its higher maximum road speed. Power for the Cromwell came from a gasoline-powered engine. (*Pierre-Olivier Buan*)

(**Opposite, above**) The British government supplied to the Soviet Union about 3,000 examples of the open-topped vehicle pictured here and referred to as the 'Universal Carrier'. Of that number, about half were Canadian-built. The maximum armour on the front of the 5ft-tall vehicle was 10mm. Its gasoline engine could provide it with a top speed on level roads of about 30mph. As one might guess, its narrow tracks did not perform well in thick mud or deep snow. (*Author's collection*)

(**Opposite, below**) The Red Army Universal Carrier pictured here is armed with a British-designed and built .55 Boys Anti-Tank Rifle. Also visible in the picture is the distinctive top-loading curved box magazine of a 7.7mm Bren light machine gun. The same machine gun also showed up as part of the standard equipment on the various British tanks supplied to the Red Army. During the war the Red Army employed the Universal Carrier as a reconnaissance vehicle and a general-purpose utility vehicle. (*Author's collection*)

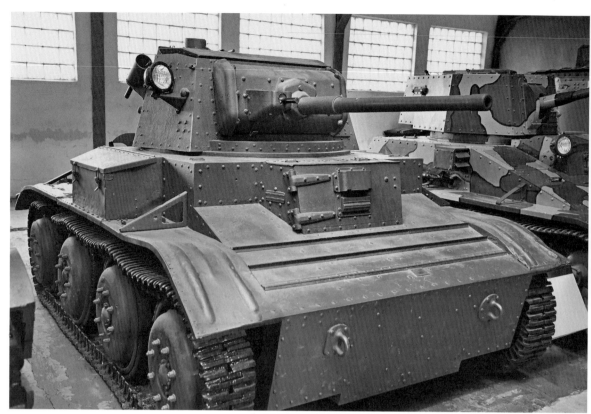

On display here at a Russian military museum is undoubtedly the only surviving example of twenty British-designed and built Light Tank Mark VII Tetrarchs delivered to the Red Army in January 1942. Armed with a 2-pounder (40mm) main gun, the maximum frontal armour thickness was 14mm. Power came from a gasoline engine that provided a top speed on level roads of 40mph. Originally intended as a reconnaissance vehicle for the British Army, it was later repurposed as an airborne tank, light enough for delivery by glider. (*Dreamstime*)

Bibliography

Drabkin, Artem, *Panzer Killers: Anti-Tank Warfare on the Eastern Front* (Pen & Sword Military, 2013).

Drabkin, Artem and Sheremet, Oleg, *T-34 in Action: Soviet Tank Troops in World War II* (Stackpole Books, 2006).

Dunn, Jr. Walter, *Hitler's Nemesis: The Red Army, 1930–45* (Stackpole Books, 1994).

Forczyk, Robert, *Panther vs T-34: Ukraine 1943* (Osprey Publishing Ltd, 2007).

Gander, Terry, *Allied Infantry Weapons of World War Two* (Crowood Press Ltd, 2000).

Harriman, Bill, *The Mosin-Nagant Rifle* (Osprey Publishing Ltd, 2016).

Hogg, Ian V., *The Encyclopedia of Infantry Weapons of World War II* (Bison Books Corp., 1984).

Hogg, Ian V., *The Illustrated Encyclopedia of Ammunition* (New Burlington Books, 1988).

Hogg, Ian V., *The Illustrated Encyclopedia of Artillery* (Chartwell Books, 1988).

Hogg, Ian V., *Allied Artillery of World War Two* (The Crowood Press Ltd, 1998).

Kavalerchik, Boris, *The Tanks of Operation Barbarossa: Soviet Versus German Armour on the Eastern* Front (Pen & Sword Limited, 2018).

Kinnear, James, *Russian Armored Cars 1930–2000* (Darlington Productions Inc., 2000).

McNab, Chris, *Soviet Submachine Guns of World War II: PPD-40, PPSh-41 and PPS* (Osprey Publishing Ltd, 2014).

Norris, John, *Infantry Mortars of World War Two* (Osprey Publishing Ltd, 2002).

Pegler, Martin, *Sniping Rifles on the Eastern Front 1939–45* (Osprey Publishing Ltd, 2019).

Rottman, Gordon L., *Soviet Rifleman 1941–45* (Osprey Publishing Ltd, 2007).

Samsonov, Peter, *Designing the T-34: Genesis of the Revolutionary Soviet Tank* (Gallantry Books, 2019).

Zaloga, Steven J., *T-34 vs StuG III: Finland 1944* (Osprey Publishing Ltd, 2019).

Zaloga, Steven J., *T-34-76 Medium Tank 1941–1945* (Osprey Publishing Ltd, 1994).

Zaloga, Steven J., *T-34-85 Medium Tank 1944–94* (Osprey Publishing Ltd, 1996).

Zaloga, Steven J., *BT Fast Tank: The Red Army's Cavalry Tank 1931–45* (Osprey Publishing Ltd, 2016).

Zaloga, Steven J., *T-26 Light Tank: Backbone of the Red Army* (Osprey Publishing Ltd, 2014).

Zaloga, Steven J. and Grandsen, James, *Soviet Tanks and Combat Vehicles of World War Two* (Arms and Armour Press, 1984).

Zaloga, Steven J. and Kinnear, Jim, *KV-1 & 2 Heavy Tanks 1939–1945* (Osprey Publishing Ltd, 1995).

Zaloga, Steven J. and Ness, Leland S., *Red Army Handbook 1939–1945* (Sutton Publishing Ltd, 1998).

Notes

Notes

Notes

Notes

Notes

Notes

Notes